T0197317

The Nature of Men and Women,

The X and Y Factor,

or

I Didn't Say it was your Fault,

I Said I was Going to Blame You

John West

authorHOUSE®

AuthorHouse™
1663 Liberty Drive
Bloomington, IN 47403
www.authorhouse.com
Phone: 1 (800) 839-8640

Published by AuthorHouse 12/14/2016

ISBN: 978-1-5246-4814-5 (sc)
ISBN: 978-1-5246-4812-1 (hc)
ISBN: 978-1-5246-4813-8 (e)

Library of Congress Control Number: 2016918204

Print information available on the last page.

This book is printed on acid-free paper.

Table of Contents

Table of Contents

Preface

After 30 years of dating and 4 wives it finally dawned on me that maybe men and women were wired differently. (I must have had a fairly flat learning curve when it came to women.) Women seem to have biological and social agendas; men do guy stuff.

"Why on earth did you do that?" was a question my current wife (and others) often asked. "Why did you do it that way?" often followed the first question. I did not understand her puzzlement. I was just doing what I do, the way I do, what I do. What did she not understand? Finally I said, "It is a guy thing. You are a female you have two X chromosomes and do things the female way. I am a guy. I have one X and one Y chromosome so I do things the guy way." That was the conversation that stimulated the idea for this book.

Wearing the same jeans several days in a row astonished my wife. Apparently women do not wear the same thing even two days in a row. And just as apparently they notice if someone else does. The concept must be inherited, or at the very least, learned at an early age. I picked up my granddaughter (who is 8 years old) from school two days in a row. I had been doing chores around the house so I happened to be wearing the same work shirt two days in a row. On the way home she said, "Grandpa, isn't that the same shirt you wore yesterday?"

I wore the same golf shirt two days in a row and my wife said, "You wore that shirt yesterday." That was not just a keen observation on her part; it carried a tone critical of my selection. Women have a knack for tonal emphasis that belies the true meaning of their comment. I said, "I know but I like this shirt and I am playing golf with different people so they won't know I wore it yesterday."

I think men get a bad rap for being men, so I want to shed some positive light on manhood. To illustrate, think about this statement and decide if you think it might be true. A husband gives his wife an unexpected gift. The first thought is what did he do or what does he want. A wife gives her husband an unexpected gift and we think, "How sweet".

Look at a dozen women's magazines, they all have articles on how to get men to change or be more romantic or learn to do the dishes. Look at a man's magazine; no articles on how to change a woman. Articles are about how to do 'guy stuff'.

I was a science teacher for over 30 years and I could see there were numerous factors that were skewed by the difference in the sex chromosomes of men and women, the X and Y chromosomes. I also realized it was millions of years of evolutionary changes in the chromosomes in the animal kingdom that had influenced human personality. I felt it was vital to men and women to understand the effects of our natural genome on our behavior. I decided to write a book that exposed the seriously funny nature of men and women. I gathered information from science text books, scientific journals, articles from newspapers, relationship sites, stories from the internet, and personal experience. Many jokes that are repeated in this book are ones I have heard over the years, ones sent by friends, jokes in magazines, and ones coming from the internet. I do not claim to be an expert on relationships (4 wives as I mentioned), I am just trying to have fun with the subject and offer a humorous semi-scientific overview of the sexes.

This book will delve into factors that make men and women act the way they do both biologically and socially. There are some original ideas and conclusions in this book and I like to think some keen observations. My wife and I have agreed that I get to do things the 'guy' way and she gets to do things the 'female' way. She isn't always pleased and I often have to hold my tongue (maybe I have learned something). I hope you enjoy my efforts as a male profiling the sexes.

Introduction

This book hopes to offer a plethora of information about the nature of men and women. It is written in a humorous and semi-scientific way so anyone can both learn and laugh at the same time.

On January 27, one billion years BCE sex began. (Actually, the exact date is hard to pinpoint so give or take a few million years, January 27, one billion years BCE is close enough.) The default sex was female; that is why men have nipples. 300 million years ago (again plus or minus a few million years) the 'Y' chromosome appeared, thus ushering in the wonder that we call male. Not long after that, the mating dance began and males and females established their roles in nature. 35,000 years ago modern humans took the stage bringing with them those inherited roles. Today, the Bettys and Bobs, the Marios and Marias, the Lars and Hannahs of the world still embrace the mating dance with the added features of emotions like love, romance, humor, and sometimes commitment.

The behaviors of the human male and the human female are affected by millions of years of animal evolution. We can see common behaviors of males throughout the animal kingdom. The same is true of females. It is not a coincidence that a male lion and male human expect the females to wait on them, bring them dinner, and take care of the kids. It is not a coincidence that male peacock and human males like to 'strut their stuff' in front of females. It is not a coincidence that human females like to 'feather' their nests. With thousands of common behaviors exhibited by both males and females along the ancestral tree of humans, common links must be acknowledged. Therefore, we will look at how the inherited genetic make-up of males and females affect the behavior of the Bobs and Bettys of today's world.

There is a joke I enjoy, men enjoy, and even women nod their heads in agreement with the message. There are many versions of this joke and thus add credibility to its message. A man, while walking along the beach, stubs his toe on something in the sand. He picks it up and brushes off the sand. It is a magic lamp, so upon brushing it, a genie pops out. However, it is an old genie. He has a long grey beard and is stooped over. "Wow," he says, "I have been stuck in that lamp for centuries. I am feeling very old and quite weak but if you have a moderate wish, I may be able to grant it for you". The man says, "I am a civil engineer. I have built roads and bridges my whole life. I would like to have a monument to my career. I wish I could build a road to Hawaii". The genie drops his head, slumps his shoulders and says, "Come on man, I said a moderate wish. Give me a break, I am weak. Surely there is something else you might wish for". "Well, there is one other thing on my mind. It is women. I say one thing and they hear something else. They say something and I always misunderstand. I do not get them. I wish I could understand women". The genie looks at him, slumps even more and says, "So, is that a two lane or a four lane bridge?"

This mating dance is confusing, frustrating, and sometimes dangerous for men and women alike. Try as they might, the Bobs and Bettys struggle to understand the natural habits of the opposite sex.

While understanding the opposite sex does not guarantee a 'happily ever after' it is the first step toward successful love and mate selection. Offered in this book are guide lines, helpful quizzes, and easy to use check lists that will help you navigate the minefield of love and marriage. The 'guy thing' is an important aspect of males. Ladies, your happiness may depend on understanding the 'guy thing'. The reverse is also true; men, catching a glimpse into the female mystique may relieve masculine frustration.

Find out what 'love' is in chapter 11. Visit the husband store and 17 pages of useful hints to 'finding a mate' in Chapter 12. See how nature and nurture play with your feelings in chapter 7. Men and women are humorously defined both biologically and socially in chapters 9 and 10. Chapter 14 includes an easy, fail-safe check list to a successful marriage. You need a sense of humor or an endless sense of compassion to compete in the human mating dance. Reading this book will give valuable insights to the nature of men and women.

Chapter 1

The Beginning of Sex

Life began quite sexless. Early organisms had no sex. There were no males, no females, no differentiation based on genitalia, behavior, or poky things. For billions of years, one celled Protozoans scurried around just trying to stay alive. One day, that changed. One day out of billions of years, one cell adhered to another cell and they swapped genetic material. They went on their way with no hug, no handshake, and no thank you; just swap and go. Protozoans do feel sensations, maybe not happiness, but something made them do it and continue to do it. Though not the beginning of sex, it was "one small step for man, and a giant leap for mankind." The exchange of genetic material proved beneficial, and a trend was born. That swap enabled the growth of diversity, and led from asexual to sexual reproduction.

Other organisms, instead of adhering to one another, began to throw out special cells that would connect and form offspring, a toss and go of genetic material. There appeared to be two different groups of the same species throwing out slightly different special cells to make a new individual. This action may have been the precursor of sex, a "pre-sex" if you will. A couple hundred millions of years later and two kinds of special cells were developing. It took about two billion years of trial and error to hit on what today is a successful strategy of egg and sperm.

What is Sex? When did it Start?

Sex revolves around methods of reproduction. Simply put, if you produce a mature special cell (gamete) to reproduce, you are a sexual organism. If there is no mature special cell, you are asexual, a no-sex organism. There are two kinds of special cells (gametes) called an egg or a sperm. If you produce an egg, you are a female. If you produce a sperm, you are a male. The coded directions for the human female or male are on the X and Y chromosomes, and therefore these chromosomes determine the sex of the individual. Interestingly, the female came first, way first. There was an intermediate form of male, a non-female, but not yet a male along the way. A lot of women think most men are an intermediate form anyway. Finally, billions of years from year zero, comes the male. Sexual reproduction started about one billion years ago.

Sexual Reproduction

Sexual organisms need the male gamete, sperm, to fertilize the female gamete, egg, in order to produce a new organism. Nowhere on earth do we find a third type of gamete (if there was a third one at one time, it did not work and it died). Whether it is a worm, a starfish, a clam, an insect, a flower, a duck-billed platypus or a human, no more than two gametes, an egg and a sperm, are needed to produce an offspring. (A threesome may produce a child but only for the fun of it).

Sex or No Sex

We have a huge diversity of life on earth. The sexual delivery system of exchanging genetic material between males and females is successful among both animals and plants. Mating rituals between animals on all levels are especially interesting. To be sure, single cell, asexual organisms still exist throughout the world as they have for billions of years. Sexual reproduction was not vital to the continuation of life on this planet. However, it seems the more ways life can reproduce the happier our evolutionary genome becomes. And for humans, sex seems to be a major driving force in our daily lives.

Gender and LGBT

Humans are not locked into a strict biological imperative of reproduction. And it seems human nature is not locked into a strict definition of gender either. LGBT stands for 'lesbian,' 'gay,' 'bisexual,' and 'transgender'. In some cases a human is born with both sexual genitalia. The term used for this is hermaphrodite and is a common occurrence in many animals and plants. According to an article in the newspaper from 11-2-13, in Germany, parents do not have to register their new-born as male or female. A gender can be decided later. The human mind is wide open to variations of sexual desire and identity. While it takes a male and female gamete to produce an offspring, it does not take 'only' the opposite sex to 'have sex'. The desire toward the opposite sex or same-sex or both sexes is quite common. One article I read mentioned as many as 1,500 animal species, males and females, have been observed engaging in same sex activities. These animals include lions and giraffes and especially herd animals. "Friends with benefits" is prevalent in non-human animals. Group groping is particularly popular, as is oral sex, among the monkey set. It appears that in many animals, same-sex (male or female) relationships prove and improve loyalty to the group, thus enabling a tighter group for hunting and defense. Many animals solve conflicts by practicing same sex activities. These relationships are not new in the biological world. Accepting these behaviors in humans is hard for some people and many of these behaviors have ignorantly been outlawed in some countries. In our world of surgical miracles, if you don't like the sex you were born with you can swap it for another. The sexual equipment door is wide open.

Any Advantage to Being Male or Female?

It would seem that the female is the more important gender, and should therefore have some life advantages or increased birth rates over the male. One male can fertilize the eggs of many females, so the world needs many strong females but only a few strong males willing to pass their sperm around. Nature always seems to find a balance. Birth statistics in the US since 1940 show five million more males have been born than females. However, females in every population, in every country, live longer than males by about five years. It would seem the role of warrior and worker (maybe a colorful decoy), while being a benefit to family and community, takes a toll on the longevity of the male population. There is slight evidence that females have more health protection than males, especially in heart matters. Nature dictates that men and women must survive long enough to reproduce, after that nature does not care. There does not seem to be any health related advantage to being male or female, unless you feel living to be one hundred is a great achievement.

Chapter 2

A Short Lesson on Genetics

If you go to any major book store and peruse the cooking section, you will see a hundred different cook books. Each has a variety of recipes. The recipes are a set of instructions for making something from a list of ingredients. That is much like genetics. Living things come with inherited instructions and their own list of ingredients. Look around the world and you can see what Mother Nature has cooked up.

Life has been around for over 3 billion years. The diversity and complexity of living organisms is immense and often beyond belief. Our discussion of genetics, inheritance, and evolution of the sexes is not meant to be all-inclusive. It is factual, but is, nevertheless, a narrow view of males and females in general.

Gregor Mendel (1822 – 1884) is considered the father of modern genetics with his laws of heredity. Charles Darwin (1809 – 1882) gave us his theory of natural selection in 1858. I find the field of genetics very interesting but also extremely complicated. Exciting discoveries seem to happen every day. While genetics unfolds some vital and amazing information, for the purposes of this book we only need to understand a few general concepts.

Living organisms may consist of one cell to hundreds of trillions of cells. In each cell there is material that guides the cell. That material is deoxyribonucleic acid or DNA. DNA contains the blueprints, the recipe, for the construction and behavior of living organisms. It does not matter whether an ant or a flower or a fish or a human, the plans for construction of each organism is in the DNA of that organism. Strands of DNA are called chromosomes. Located on sections of the chromosome are areas called genes. The gene is responsible for one step in the process of the blueprint. The sum total of all the genes located on all the chromosomes of an organism is called its genome. What is really cool is that in all living organisms the genetic material, the DNA, has essentially the same basic formula. Only the sequence and length of the parts of DNA are different from organism to organism.

Scientists from the" Human Genome Project", completed in 2003, have been able to map every gene in the human genome. We humans have an estimated 20,500 genes scattered around our 46 (23 pairs) chromosomes.

One of the concepts I want you to remember is that genes, in all organisms, are inherited from parents/ancestors. That means instructions for construction are passed from generation to generation. The offspring inherits its traits from the chromosomes/ genes passed to it from its parents. This is where Gregor Mendel did his experiments and established some laws of heredity.

Another concept vital to our discussion is that genes change, and that change is passed to the offspring. There are several ways a gene may change. It is not important for us to know or understand the how and why of gene mutation, only that it does happen, and has for billions of years. Further, genes are blind to the future. That means the change may be good, bad, or neutral. If the change helps survival of the offspring then the gene stays in the genome and in the gene pool of living organisms. That would be a successful gene. If the change is bad and the offspring does not survive that gene hits a dead end (a little pun). A neutral change just goes along for the ride. This is where Charles Darwin explained his laws of natural selection. This successful change of living organisms over time is called evolution.

Most of the 20,000 + genes that humans have are also found in other animals throughout the animal kingdom. Examples are genes that make bones, skin, muscle, and internal organs. Obviously humans have some new genes or we would not be a separate species. Essentially our genes have been passed up the evolutionary ladder from other animals to us humans. Some of our genes are billions of years old; some are only several thousand years old. We do in fact share over 99% of our genes with the chimpanzee. (The old saying, "I'll be a monkey's uncle" should be, "I'll be a monkey's nephew".)

John West

Let's talk specifically about human reproduction, and inheritance. Humans have 23 pairs of chromosomes, 46 in all. 23 come from mom and 23 come from dad. The passing of chromosomes occurs during reproduction. 23 chromosomes are in the sperm and 23 chromosomes are in the egg. When the two gametes unite, an offspring with 46 chromosomes begins with half its instructions from mom and half its instructions from dad (sometimes causing no end of confusion).

The chromosomes in humans are numbered 1 – 23. The 23rd chromosome is the sex chromosome, and is called 'X' or 'Y'. One sex chromosome from each parent is passed to the offspring. In humans, the recipe for a male is X and Y, while the one for the female is X and X. Two things become obvious. First is the male has only one X, while the female has 2 Xs. Secondly, the male has a Y chromosome and the female has no Y chromosome. It is amazing how an X or Y can create such a different outcome.

To summarize: every cell contains material that guides the cell, that material is DNA. DNA contains the instructions for construction and behavior of an organism. Strands of DNA are called chromosomes, and sections of the chromosome are called genes. Genes control one step of the overall program, genes are passed (inherited) to the offspring, genes can change, and some genes are immortal. From the "Human Genome Project", we learned that humans carry over 20,000 genes. These genes were inherited from our ancestors over millions of years. Men and women are different by a factor of X or Y.

Insanity is inherited; you get it from your kids.

Chapter 3

The Gene Pool

Now that you have a basic understanding of chromosomes, genes, and the genome it is time to discuss the 'gene pool'. The gene pool of life consists of all the genes that are alive and functioning today in all living things. That is a big pool. Generally speaking, today's pool is made up of many individual pools. The human gene pool has many of the same genes as all life forms, but we also have some genes specific only to humans. Men and women have their specific genes also, hence the Bettys and Bobs, and the Isadores and Isabellas of the world.

There we are, all living things bobbing up and down in life's pool. It would be nice if the pool were chlorinated, but it's not. It is a messy conglomeration of all biting, sucking, stinging, chewing and licking organisms. Every now and then, one of the groups gets pulled out and disappears. Occasionally some new thing jumps in.

Tough Enough

Our human genes are tough survivors. They have fought and lived to tell their tale. They are here because they work, they are successful, and they promote our species. There are ancient genes in this human pool and there are new genes in our pool. The guard in this pool does not allow any mistakes. If you die before you pass your genes to an offspring your genes are pulled from the pool and are gone forever. Most guards at a pool jump in to save a struggling person; just the opposite happens in life's gene pool. If you cannot survive on your own, your loser genes are pulled from the pool and thrown away, (and I thought water polo was tough.) Unfortunately, there are some vicious genes in our pool that I would like to see 'drowned' or 'yanked' from the pool, but they are tough survivors themselves. (Do we really need mosquitos?)

Darwin Awards

Darwin is generally given credit for the idea of 'survival of the fittest' as an aspect of evolution. On a somewhat dark humorous note, each year a list of 'Darwin' awards are given out. A group looks at the dumbest way an individual has died due to his or hers own folly. These genes are thus eliminated from the human gene pool before they can be passed on to another generation. This in turn is supposed to help the human advance as a more successful species with the removal of these 'folly' genes. There does not seem to be any benefit for carrying 'folly' genes, yet they show up year after year, and seem to be a human invention. Rarely do we see 'lower' animals involved with dare devil stunts. There is the occasional taunting and teasing of one animal to another in what appears to be animal humor. (I saw one video of a young monkey teasing young lions by hanging from a tree and pulling their tails.) Often times the winners of these awards have consumed large amounts of alcohol and there is some sort of live-or-die contest involved. Shooting an apple off one's head with a hunting bow and arrow comes to mind. Breaking into animal cages at the zoo is another award winner. Knives, guns, and explosives are frequently involved. Racing a train to a crossing may be a lethal event. Testing a used gas mask with lethal gas should be a no-no. Making a pipe bomb from a book is another mistake. For years only men achieved honors for the top ten Darwin awards, but lately women have found themselves award winners. There seems no end to the extent of what can only be called D.F.S. or 'dumb fucking stunts'. Trying to find an adequate adjective for ultimate stupidity is difficult. People can take themselves out of the human gene pool in amazingly, stupefying, absurd, inane, and insane ways. There are several web sites one can search with lists of dumb crooks, dumb stunts, and dumb ways that can cause injuries and extinction.

Mass Extinction

Millions of organisms that were once successful have been yanked out of the gene pool. Mass extinctions are still a puzzle to biologists. Whatever the reason, at least 70% of once living organisms have become extinct. Their unique genes were lost from the gene pool forever. The most commonly known extinction is that of the dinosaurs. The point I am making is that only the organisms that survive pass on their genes to future generations. When you think of all the events that have occurred on Earth over 4 billion years, the road to today's living organisms is really a kind of 'pin-ball' route.

Odd Genes

Presumably the genes in the human gene pool have some evolutionary benefit to humans. There are, however, humorous and not-so-helpful genes in the pool. What is up with being ticklish? What kind of advantage is that? Nerve endings that send a signal to your brain that stimulate a wiggle and a giggle? Then why can't you tickle yourself? Does spasmodic laughing help produce offspring? Humans carry left over genes from the past; ones that helped out our ancestors several million years ago but are no longer of use today. These may produce vestigial organs; examples are the appendix, wisdom teeth, tail bone, a third eye lid, and muscles to wiggle your ears.

Bummer Genes

Apparently there are genes in our pool that turn humans old. We have these great successful survivor genes only to have them break down and die. Fungus lives longer than we do. I was talking to a friend of mine and I asked him about the evolutionary advantage to us turning bald and gray. He pointed out that turning bald and gray was an advantage to ovulating women and our predators, not to men. Predators stalking the herds for prey can see the bald and gray members and know that they are the slower and weaker ones.

In another cruel twist, being gray tells the young females looking for a big healthy sperm to not bother with the old guys. The old guys should not be reproducing so they are shunned by the chicks and predators can "glean" them from the pack.

Our genes are in the pool for better or worse, so we are what we are. Humans are the end product of several billion years of evolution. Maybe we are a humorous byproduct of genetic mistakes? Ladies, is that ogling, drooling guy next to you in a bar really at the top of the evolutionary tree? Looking at the behavior of some of the people around us we must wonder, "What were those genes thinking?"

Chapter 4

The Delivery System

As mentioned earlier, sex began when two organisms sidled up together and swapped genetic material. Millions of years later, organisms developed special cells that could unite with other special cells. Fertilization is the process in which two gametes (sex cells) unite to form a new individual. How these gametes meet with one another depends on the delivery system.

Early life began in water. In water the male gamete (sperm) just floated toward the female. The female had means to capture the male gamete and match it up with its gamete (egg). As long as the organisms were in the water the delivery system could be called 'floaters' or 'drifters'. With animals that did not move, like coral or clams for example, the drift system was in play. With animals that moved the female might lay a clutch of eggs and the male would swim over the clutch and squirt the sperm onto the eggs. Genetic memory guided each sex to its specific acts.

On land, the plants used a similar system of floating the sperm into the air and having the female catch it with some kind of sticky bloom. Plants have also evolved a timing factor for reproduction. Sperm release is spread out over several months. Some plants are early spring while others are late fall.

Hermaphrodites

One interesting reproduction adaptation I might mention is the earthworm. The earthworm, like many other animals, is hermaphroditic. They contain both sex organs and produce both male and female gametes. That adaptation is very handy while crawling through the ground. No matter who you meet, you can mate. That is a very successful adaption for reproduction.

Penile Bone

A land animal male could not rely on throwing his sperm into the air and hoping a female was in the neighborhood to catch it. Land animals developed a delivery system of personal contact. Essentially the male would search out a female and deliver his sperm personally. That delivery system involves a male rod for insertion, usually called a "penis" into a female opening, usually called a "vagina." Most male placental mammals also have a penile bone, a baculum, or "Os Penis". The bone is found in carnivores, rodents, bats and primates like the old world monkeys and apes. One can readily see how a penile bone would help the process of insertion in order to personally deliver the sperm. The down side to that is care must be taken not to accidentally injure or break the bone. Any insertion efforts with a broken bone(r) would be futile.

Size Matters

There is evidence that female muskrats use size of penis (with bone) as an indicator of male 'quality'. Animals that mate underwater (seals for example) also use size as a measure of 'quality'. In bats, males mate with females who are hibernating. This seems sneaky to me but a good penile bone does get the job done. The penile bone varies a lot in size and shape. There does not seem to be a clear reason for this variety.

No Bone for Humans

Not all placental animals have an 'Os Penis'. You may have noticed the penile bone is missing in human males. Seems like a good reproduction idea, but evidently humans did not need one to reproduce. Still, why not? In humans Richard Dawkins, an evolutionary biologist, has proposed that the "baculum" disappeared by female selection. Unlike the bats, the human female mated with the lights on so to speak. Females pick strong, healthy males as mating partners to insure strong, healthy offspring. If not for this fact, life as we know it would not be here today. It may be that the woman was not interested in an artificial boner. She wanted the real thing. Disease and old age among other things will affect the hardness of an erection. A good, hard, large erection is an indication of healthy and viable sperm and therefore is an attractive asset for the male. "If you can't get it up, I don't want it," may have been the attitude of the evolutionary female. Once the bone gene was dropped from the human gene pool, it was never to be seen again. Of course modern science has brought back the artificial boner with certain drugs.

The Mammal Egg Hunt

While the male fires out his sperm, the female holds in her eggs. The eggs are produced internally and fertilized internally for placental mammals. The eggs are in a nice warm place. The vagina offers a nice passageway to carry the sperm to a meeting with the egg. It is important for the male to have a forceful ejection to insure the delivery of the sperm to the inner areas of the egg's location. The male climax lets him know his sperm are on their way, and the erection softens. Without a good climax, the male could walk away before the job was done. It is an added bonus that the signal that the sperm have been released, the climax, delivers a nicely pleasurable feeling. After all, if the male found no joy in spreading his sperm, mating would be chancy and the species would die out. A climax for a female was not important or necessary; she had to wait for the male sperm to arrive whether she was breathing hard or not. The satisfaction for the female is knowing her eggs would be fertilized. There are also some pleasure nerve endings at the vagina to ensure a willingness to mate. As nature would have it, the penis of each male species fits the opening and position of the female of the same species. The female wants to have all her eggs fertilized. She does not get an erection for mating, her opening is passive. That means she can collect as much sperm as she wants from multiple partners to insure a fertilized egg. (Bees and termites are famous for this.)

Mating Rituals and Mate Selection

As long as the world has had males and females, the process of mate selection has occurred. For the most part the story line for millions of years is that the females pick the mate. The male does his dance and the female picks her partner. It must be noted that at no time, no-where, has the male ever figured out how the selection process works. What we know is the female wants to have babies. They know it takes a male and they know most males will die to mate.

Timing is Everything

Placental females do not produce eggs by the millions. It takes a specific period of time for the eggs to develop. Most mammals want to give birth during the spring when abundant food is available for the offspring. So, depending on gestation period, females have a specific time period when eggs will be available for fertilization. Naturally the females want the males to know when it is time to mate. There are several signals the female will send out. Pheromones are the primary signal. Pheromones are molecules of odor. A male can sniff out that scent blocks away, through a brick wall, or across the room in a smoky bar. Another signal may be a change in skin color. Males can see and smell the invitation for intercourse. Human women's signals are more subtle than a pink butt or some musky odor, but still, signals are sent and pheromones do flow. Human females have eggs ready any time of the year, but usually available only once month. Interestingly enough, the months with the most human births are July, August and September, in that order. If you count back nine months you see winter is when most conceptions occur (makes sense). I am just guessing, but New Year's Eve may set the record for conceptions.

Clitoris

Another major step in human evolution is the female clitoris. (The clitoris is also found in many mammals, and a limited number of other animals.) It is often likened to the male penis in that it contains many pleasure nerve endings, as many as 8000. It is necessary for the vagina to be lubricated for the penis injection. Stimulating the clitoris, and other means of sexual arousal, helps the process of lubricating the vaginal walls. In most cases the stimulation will bring a feeling of excitement to the woman. While the climax in men is almost universally pleasurable, not all women get a climax or heightened pleasure through intercourse alone.

Human Pleasure

Humans will simulate the steps necessary for reproduction just for fun. Having sex is fun. It is believed that only humans (and maybe Bonobos) have sex just for fun. When it comes to sex, humans have evolved past the basic animal need to reproduce. It appears that any time is a good time for sex.

Chapter 5

Genetic Memory, Part 1

The cool thing about a living organism is that it can learn from experience. If that experience helps it to survive, then those memories can be encoded in the genome on the genes. Those genes then determine behavior based on those coded memories. Additional learning through the years can modify the genes or the action of the genes. Genes can be turned on, turned off, turned down, enhanced, and even mutated by the environment. Offsprings inherit the genes, the learned memories, from their parents. That way, each new and more complex organism does not have to start from square one and try to relearn a million years of experience. The behavior an animal inherits from its parents is called "instinct" or unconscious behavior. Ants, termites, and bees/wasps are perfect examples of being born knowing what to do. These animals have a very highly organized society and yet every new hatch knows exactly what its role is in the society. Humans also have quite a store of memories in their 46 chromosomes, 3 billion base pairs, and about 21,000 genes.

This chapter contains some dramatic concepts about the connections of today's men and women with their ancestral parents. We have direct parental chromosomal links to the 'first humans'. Starting with today's humans, let's travel back a few hundred thousand years.

We do not usually think of ourselves as being half mom and half dad, but the chromosomes and genes that make up who we are come directly from our mom and dad. Further, barring a genetic miss-hap, exactly half come from mom and exactly half come from dad. We like to think of ourselves as special and unique, but our personal genome was carried around by two other people years before we had it.

We need to realize too, that mom and dad each received their genes from their parents, your grandma and grandpa. That means your genes came from your grandparents. They passed through your parents right on to you. One fourth of the genes you carry around, the genes that make you who you are, came from each of your four grandparents. You can see how there may be a physical resemblance throughout a family. Some people have traced their family tree (genes) back hundreds of years. The genes you carry now, given to you from ancestors, are centuries old. If you continue to look back thousands and tens of thousands of years you realize that some of the genes you carry today are the same ones the very first humans carried. The genes that make up your bones, muscles, internal organs, senses, etc. are the same as the first humans. Interesting, but there is more! Where did that ancient Betty and ancient Bob get his/her genes?

God Given Genes?

55% of Americans will tell you that God made humans just as we exist today. Well, if that is so, he used the same genes that were already in the animal life gene pool. Humans have genes that form a backbone just like all other vertebrates. We have genes that make the same eye balls and hair and four chambered hearts and mammary glands as other mammals. We have five fingers, five toes and opposable thumbs just like all primates. Men have an X and a Y chromosome and women have two X chromosomes just like males and females of all the vertebrates. It does not take too much imagination to understand that all living things share a similar DNA/ chromosomal make-up.

Obviously, the number of chromosomes and combination of genes has changed and evolved over the past few hundred million years but the common links between humans and other vertebrates is also just as obvious.

The point of this history of the human gene is to point to the history of the human gene. We are not a stand-alone life form. Human genes and human behavior did not sprout up overnight independent of other living species on Earth. The biological and social imperatives of the vertebrates, mammals, and primate animals are carried over into humans. Male and female animals have their roles in the life scheme and those same roles are evident in human men and women. I call this roll over of roles from 'lower' animals into human behavior a genetic memory. One need only look around to see that humans have a lot of the animal instincts and behaviors in common.

Genetic Memory, Part 2

The Y Chromosome

Here is one of those dramatic concepts I mentioned in the beginning of this chapter. We know the Y chromosome is needed to make a male and the Y chromosome comes from the father only, never from the mother. The mother carries two X chromosomes so she cannot pass a Y to her offspring. The interesting thing about the Y chromosome is that it is unchanged when passed from father to son. Since the Y chromosome is passed only from male to male, the son receives the exact same Y chromosome with the same genes that made up the father. The Y is not influenced by the female (mother) in any way. Looking further, that means all brothers in a family also have the exact same copy of dad's Y. In fact all uncles and nephews have the exact same copy of the Y chromosome. Essentially, you can trace the same Y chromosome through thousands of dads through thousands of years, unchanged. Conceptually, your ancestral dad, from 10,000 years ago, and you have the exact same Y chromosome.

Modern Man

Modern man is approximately 35,000 years old. The Y chromosome may have changed somewhat in those 35,000 years, but not much. I find it interesting to think my Y chromosome was perhaps carried by a Roman solider or an African explorer.

Mitochondrial Eve

There is an interesting female to female link that can be traced back tens of thousands of years. I need to introduce another biological term at this time. There is a little 'organelle' that exists in most cells called a mitochondrion. It is sometimes called the powerhouse of the cell because its function is to break down food bits into energy for the cell. There may be as many as 1700 in a cell. The gist of the link is that the mitochondrion has its own DNA apart from the human DNA. That DNA is passed on the X chromosome to the offspring, therefore there is no male influence. One set of researchers claimed they found the most recent common female ancestor of all human beings currently in existence by tracing the mitochondria DNA link. They called her "Mitochondrial Eve". Other research has been done with similar results but different time stamps. However, the female to female links have been verified. The research does offer conclusive evidence that females today are directly linked to females hundreds of thousands of years old.

Hard Wired

Humans are hard wired by their genome with very ancient survival and instinctual memories. When Betty looks in the mirror she sees today's Betty. What she doesn't see are the genes passed to her from ancient Betty. There is another factor influencing maleness and femaleness around the world. That factor is geographic breeding groups. If, within one ethnic group, people only mate with members of its own group the genomes have little variety. This may create ethnic stereotypes.

If we summarize the genetic memories mentioned in part one and part two, we see a straight line link with behaviors of earlier animals and early humans to modern human men and women.

Chapter 6

A Box of Chocolates

When I was young, my mother would bring home a box of Sees chocolates at Xmas. Most of the fillings I did not like, however, some I did like. If I took a bite of one I had to eat the whole thing. I could not put half a chocolate back in its little wrapper in its tray. I hesitated to try one because if I did not like the filling I was stuck eating the whole thing. (Only later in life did I realize I could have just thrown the thing away.) I decided I could poke the bottom to see what the filling was like. That way, if I didn't like the filling I could put the candy back in the box, and I assumed no one would know the difference. Over the years, no one ever mentioned the poked bottoms, so I guess my plan worked.

People are like a box of chocolates, so many different varieties. They may look alike outside but inside the filling may be nutty or creamy. You can be sure that some people have fillings you are not going to like. Will Rogers said he never met a man he didn't like, but I can tell you I have met both men and women I didn't like. And as hard as it is to say, I think the feelings of some of these people were mutual.

Finding Your Match

After reading the last chapter we know that men and women may look alike on the outside, but with such an assortment of inherited genes the 'insides' are going to be very different. The fortunate thing about this variety of men and women is that no matter who you are, you are likely to find someone you can relate to. Like the box of chocolates, you will find a filling you like. However, there will be a lot of non-matches. There will be a lot of candies put back in the box with bites out of them. There will be a lot of candies thrown away. There will be a lot heart-break.

John West

Variety, a Strange Spice

Romance may be like a square dance; changing partners, do-si-dos, promenades, and dressed for fun. A caller (genome) is giving directions, sometimes easy and sometimes quick and confusing. It takes a lot of practice to get the steps and then the square changes, the caller changes, and more confusion sets in. Some people will just sit out of the dance while others rush to join in. Do not sit out, at least poke a bottom (not literally).

When I was in school we had a 'Snowball' dance. One couple would start to dance. A minute later each person would go pick someone else to dance with then those four would pick someone else and so on until the whole room was dancing. The most we can hope for in our romantic life is that, during life's Snowball dance, we get a partner or two with whom we want to dance the night away. And when that is done take him/her home and live mostly happily ever after. Maybe your favorite chocolate comes with nougat, maybe caramel, maybe coconut, but given enough chocolates you might learn to enjoy a variety of fillings.

Chapter 7

Nature vs. Nurture

Nature and nurture are important aspects of human behavior. They directly affect our relationships and personal expectations. Knowing the implications of "what comes naturally" and what can be nurtured is vital to understanding men and women. How much of human behavior is due to nature, and how much is due to having been nurtured in a particular way, is the question. A lot of books and theories have been written on this subject. Whole fields of psychology are devoted to this question. And, not surprisingly, experts are lined up in each corner with their studies and findings. Are the behaviors of men and women already determined by their respective genomes? Do 'guy' things come naturally or are they learned? Can a good woman's love change a man's disposition? Can a man make a woman love him? Why do some women go for the 'dangerous/bad boy' while others want a 'comfortable man'?' Is that natural? If you want to understand and comprehend men or women you need to know their nature and the possible effects of nurture.

Nature Driven

What does nature driven mean? It means the genes each one of us inherits determine behavior. It means we are born with pre-determined patterns, pre-set actions and reactions to our environment. The brain is not a clean slate, but a carefully scripted novel that has been preinstalled by our genome. We have a biological imperative that drives our actions. We have instincts. Survival and security are first. Reproduction is second. For most organisms there is no third. Humans have emotional instincts that are not found in 'lower animals'. Our cerebral cortex differentiates us from other animals, but may be somewhat preprogramed through 40,000 years of "Humanness". If we are genetically driven we may have little control over our natural actions. The genes are in charge and the body is a container to carry them around. Human nature is the sum total of the thousands of genes passed to us over the past billion years.

Nurture Driven

Nurture driven means that while we have obvious physical inheritance, our behaviors are learned. Some behaviors are learned early, starting in the womb. Humans are born with a clean mental slate upon which nurture writes the rules of behavior. It is your parents, family life, and your personal environment (culture) that determines most of your behavior. Love and care will shape human actions. The reverse is also true; hate and neglect will also shape actions. The adult can learn and reason and is therefore in control of behaviors. Human nature is the sum total of thousands of years of learned behavior taught by society.

Look Around, Nature Rules

If you look around at the world it is obvious that nature rules the actions of all non-human animals. They work strictly on instincts, their inherited behaviors. A baby turtle, upon being hatched, immediately runs for the water. Look at any adult animal in the wild; it acts according to its 'nature'. Its 'nature' is its inherited behavior, its genome. Wolverines are aggressive. Deer are extremely alert to sounds and movements and quickly run away from threats. Rarely do we see an animal, a non-human act differently from its inherited nature. That is, a coyote will always act like a coyote. A snake will always act like a snake.

There are a lot of folk tales about the behavior of animals. One was even made into a song. A woman found a snake cold and nearly frozen outside her house. Feeling compassionate she brought the snake inside the house and put it by the fire to warm up. Eventually the snake warmed up and moved its muscles. It looked at the woman and asked why she had helped him. She simply said she felt sorry for his plight and wanted to help. She approached the snake to comfort it and it struck out and bit her. She yelled and shrunk back asking why, after she had brought him in from the cold, fed him and cared for him, had he bitten her. He replied, "Because I am a snake, that is what I do". (In the song the snake may have symbolized a man and she as a naïve woman.)

Humans are Animals

Most people like to think humans are different from lower animals but humans were not just brought by the stork as totally independent from the rest of the animal world. Humans operate on the same animal genes that were inherited over millions of years. Another often heard phrase is 'human nature'. Remember, nature means inherited characteristics.

Up the Ladder

The combination of the human brain and cerebral cortex does move humans up the evolutionary ladder a few rungs above the ordinary animal, implying behaviors that are a few steps above the reptilian/instinct-only actions of the 'lower' animals. (Although after several beers, the human male can slip a few rungs downward on the ladder and they can turn quite 'beastly'.) Does this advanced brain affect the 'nature vs nurture' dynamic? Is it nature or nurture that most influences human behavior? Is Betty or Bob free to act on feelings, or are they genetically controlled? There are excellent studies that help to answer that question.

Identical Twins

Identical twins come from a single fertilized egg that has split in two resulting in two humans with the exact same genetic make-up. That is to say, their nature is the same. What do you think would happen if identical twins were separated at birth and grew up in different 'nurture' environments? That outcome would certainly shed light on the question of 'nature vs nurture'. If you search the internet for identical twins separated at birth you will find numerous stories and studies. One such study was launched in 1979 at the University of Minnesota. The study involved about 60 pairs of identical twins who were separated at birth. Remarkable similarities were found. Behaviors were the same, medical histories were the same, habits and hobbies were the same; even the same cars were preferred. In one example of male twins, they had both married women named Linda, divorced and married women named Betty, had named their sons James Allan, and had dogs named 'Toy'. Estimates of 'sameness' ranged from 60% to 75% throughout the many twin studies. While this is not a totally conclusive study it gives a strong indication more than half of one's behavior is genetically controlled.

Siblings

The flip side to twins separated at birth is siblings growing up together. In this case the genes are different but the environment is the same. That is to say life-style is the same, while the genome is different. Even a casual look at families will show brothers and sisters in large or small families developing different behaviors. Several books have been written about 'the middle child', 'the first child,' and 'the youngest child,' all trying to explain the difference in behaviors. Apparently, in the same 'nurture' environment, different behaviors occur. It seems nature may have more of an effect on human behavior than nurture.

Chips and Blocks

Often used phrases like 'a chip off the ole block' and 'bad blood runs in that family,' are anecdotal observations that also agree with gene controlled behavior.

Gender Differences

Further evidence of behavior controlled by genes is found in gender differences. We see the mammalian/primate roles of behavior of males and females are clearly different. General observation of animal nature suggests that sexual roles across the board are fairly consistent in actions. Men and women are inherently different. Males, in general, act like males; they do not act like females. The reverse is also true.

The Nurture Effect

It is evident that the genome exerts considerable controls on an individual. It sets the development of the brain and its ability to learn. But the modern human is more complicated, with a larger brain than primitive humans or lower animals. The nurture effect may layer with the genome. Humans are affected by their environment, their culture. The genome is the operating system but the environment can turn the volume up or down, adjust the focus, tune or modify the genes. It is like putting upholstery on a chair, or putting a design in the fabric. Nurture is like accessorizing your genetic wardrobe.

Frontal Lobe of the Cerebral Cortex

The frontal lobe is the area of the brain that controls many emotions. It may also take 24 to 30 years to mature. This is another good reason to wait until the late twenties to try to form a permanent relationship. Anything earlier and you do not know what you are getting in the deal; don't start playing the hand until all the cards are dealt.

Nurturing effects take place in the frontal lobe of the brain. This is the area of the brain where you fix your value system, your conscience, judgment, and your morals. It is where you store ideas of right and wrong, recognition, memory, and 'civilized' behavior. Nurture affects our social behavior. Humans can be more than a naked ape. It is the development of the frontal cortex that really separates humans from the rest of the animal kingdom.

Relationships and Nurture

Nurturing helps people build their relationships with other people. This idea is vital to the success of male-female connections. People have the ability to enjoy life, sense pleasure, become emotional, and love one another when properly nurtured. Nurturing will not make you any smarter, any faster, and any more talented but it will help you enjoy your life and friendships and achieve your personal potential. The way you are nurtured affects the way you treat other people.

Optimism

One redeeming feature of humans is their sense of optimism. Most people think they are adaptable, they think change is possible. That is why there is a huge market for self-help books. It spawns the whole psychology, psychiatry, 'search for enlightenment' thing. And why a woman will marry a man thinking she can change him? One standard joke goes "A woman marries a man thinking he will change. A man marries a woman hoping she won't change". Getting married a second or third time is the triumph of hope over reality.

Summary

Understanding the effects of nature and nurture will give valuable insights to relationship possibilities. Whether we are run mostly by nature (genes) or nurture (learned behavior) or equally by both, by the time we are adults our behaviors are nearly fixed. We are who we are. What you see is what you get. Your genes are not going to change. Your learned culture has already been ingrained. There may be a spot in your brain for some new learned behaviors, but that is probably a tiny spot. People are not much more adaptable than that. The insight here is, never go into a relationship thinking you are going to change another person's behavior. Short of a 'gene exchange' that person's blue print is fixed, done, built. Have you ever tried to live in a house while a major remodel is taking place and half way through you ran out of money? That is what it would be like trying to do a makeover on another person. Forget the remodel; keep moving until you find someone you like and someone who likes you.

Chapter 8

If It Looks Like a Duck

This book is about the nature of men and women. Can we know what is true or false about men and women or maybe mostly true sometimes but not true other times? Human behavior is not an exact science so truths can be conditional and conclusions may be apparent but not necessarily a scientific fact.

Human behavior can be measured, observed, studied, recorded, analyzed and compared but in many ways still remain mysteriously inconsistent. However, we can make general statements based on observations (anecdotal evidence) that may be accepted as true. The nature of men and women draws a lot of comparisons and conclusions from scientific facts, biological natural history, evolution, patterns in human behavior, surveys and primate research (all of which can be found in some creative internet searches).

Inductive Logic

Using inductive logic, we can use specific facts to form a general statement, and we can use observations to recognize recurring patterns. From recurring patterns we can extrapolate further to make predictions. That is how this book is able to describe the nature of men and women with acceptable accuracy. To give an example of inductive logic, if it looks like a duck, walks like a duck and sounds like a duck, then it must be a duck. Inductive logic allows one to take known evidence and predict, or extrapolate, a conclusion from that evidence. This is just one means of quantifying a truth.

Bell Curve

One measuring tool that is quite useful in describing patterns of behavior is the bell curve. A bell curve illustrates the probable distribution of human mental and physical variations. Very often we put things on a scale of 1 to 10, 1 being the least and 10 being the most. If we took a sample of 1000 men throughout the country and measured their sex drive we would find a few with very little sex drive on the scale at number 1 and a few with vigorous sex drive at number 10. The majority of men (60%) would cluster on numbers 4, 5, and 6. This is how we determine the average and median of any behavior. If we did a similar sample for women charting their desire to have babies, the result might form a bell curve: little or no desire on number 1 with desire increasing each number until number 10, the woman who wants to be a walking, talking baby factory. The majority of woman (60%) would be on numbers 4, 5, and 6. Therefore, when a behavior is attributed to women (X and X chromosomes) or to men (X and Y chromosome) that means they exhibit the behavior to varying degrees, with the majority in the middle. One caveat is some humans' exhibit extreme anomalies that put them off the chart. (So when I say 'all' men/women, that really is about 95%).

Stereotypes

The bell curve may also describe a typical stereotype. For example, a bell curve of men endangering themselves in careless acts would show at one end of the curve the 'never' take a chance guy. The curve would then progress with the 'increasingly-taking-chances' guys. Eventually we get the number 10 guys, the adrenaline junkies. We see the men on numbers 5, 6,7,8,9, and 10 because they are the ones out in the public doing crazy stuff. That gives the impression that men frequently endanger themselves. While 40% or so of men do not take dumb chances, we see the 50% to 60% of men out doing crazy stuff and so a stereotype is born.

John West

Stereotypes may be semi-real and can be used in many jokes especially ones about males and females. Cartoons and comic strips and comedians rely on stereotypes to be funny. 'Andy Capp' is an English, beer drinking, soccer player who works at not working and lives off his wife 'Flo'. (The name "Andy Capp" is a phonetic rendition of the word 'handicap.') That strip started in 1957 and 59 years later is still going strong. There is even a bronze statue of Andy, unveiled in 2007, in Hartlepool, England. In this book, I may allude to stereotypes for humor's sake.

Natural History

Looking throughout the natural history of living organisms, many relevant conclusions can be made about relationships between animals and humans. It is an easy step to predict that human behavior patterns will be similar to animal patterns.

So when I say, "if it looks like duck, sounds like a duck, and walks like a duck," it must be a duck. If it acts like a jerk and sounds like a jerk, then it is probably a jerk. Very often, 'probably' is enough evidence on which to make a decision.

Chapter 9

What is a Man?

Men may seem simple to define, but there are a lot of criteria to consider. The standard used for judgment must be decided along with the question of who is doing the judging. I am sure the opinions of women would be very different from those of men. A woman might define a man by his actions, wants and desires, emotions, goals, habits, appetite, humor, strength, voice, fashion sense, character, stature, color of hair, sexual abilities, looks, or a hundred other traits that seem to be important to her. A man being judged by other men need only be a good friend, be a team player, (loyal) and buy beer when it is his turn. (A man does not come home one night. The next morning he tells his wife that he had slept over at a friend's house. The woman calls 10 of her husband's best friends. Eight confirm that he had slept over, and two say he is still there.) Men want to be judged fairly, but the rules keep changing either by women or by society; it gets frustrating.

Scientific Description

Let's start with a scientific definition of man. Man is a member of Homo sapiens with a genome that includes a 'Y' chromosome. He is a vertebrate/mammal/primate/hominid with an opposable thumb. Men produce a reproductive cell called a sperm. Men are not women. A man is the end product of millions of years of evolutionary male commandments. He is the combination of his ancestral genes rolled into a walking, talking 'phenom'.

Penis

Before we get into observable types of men and their behaviors, one very important, vitally important, aspect of man must be mentioned. Men have a penis. An appendage that makes him king of the jungle. Sometimes it is called a dick, a pee pee, peter, pecker, wiener or wienie, tube steak, swinging sirloin, trouser trout, and salami, "as in trying to hide the salami." If it is hard then it is called an erection, a boner, a woody or Mister Woody, a stiffy or Mister Stiffy. Actually any rigid object preceded by the word 'mister' will do. Pole, mast, yard arm, monolith, rocket, bazooka, etc., are samples of rigid objects that can be preceded by the word 'Mister'. Some men have special pet names for their dick. Ask your boyfriend or husband what he named his pee pee. (It is said that men are either hungry or horny. If you see a man without an erection, make him a sandwich).

An exterior appendage, that can hang out, go up or down with a look or a thought, is awesome. A man has the world in his hands. He can write his name in the snow. He has a hat or towel rack while standing up. With a pair of roller skates on he can be a pull toy. A swelling in his loins is a feeling that makes the world go around. (This may be the origin of the phrase, "Swell with Pride".) A woman may have a similar feeling when she gets wet, but with her there is no big bulge, no loud bugle, and no exclamation point that trumpets the arrival of 'Mister Woody'. From the time he experiences his first burst of hormones and wet dream to the time he has out lived his pecker, a man is pretty much driven by his crotch. When the zipper goes down, all reason dissolves. It does a man no good to have two heads.

A man had won a lotto prize of a million dollars but not long afterward he was broke. A friend asked him what had happened to his money. He said, "I spent most of it on women and booze. The rest of it I just wasted."

Penis Facts

1. According to a study in the Journal of Sexual Medicine done in 2013, 1661 men surveyed found the average erect penis was 5.5 inches (14 cm) long. The range was 1.6 inches to 10.2 inches.

2. Smoking can shorten the average penis by .4 inches due to restricted blood flow.

3. The pre-human male had a penis with spines. That condition is still found on tom cats. Fortunately the human male missed out on what certainly would have been a scary adaptation.

4. The penis works out at night. Most men have 3 to 5 erections at night. Just like any work out, this action keeps the member in shape. (This can be quite dangerous if 'Big John' rolls over quickly at night.)

Sperm Facts

There are some suggested procedures to insure stronger, faster sperm. From an article by Dr. Oz in the Arizona Republic, May 2, 2016, comes the following list: wear boxers and sleep naked, cut back on caffeine, take multi-vitamins, relax, unplug your cell phone before using, and skip smoking.

Testosterone

Along with having a penis, the Y chromosome also generates testosterone. Testosterone is the 'T' in TNT. It is the octane that changes regular into super. It is the trigger of all things brave and stupid. Testosterone primes the pump with a heady mixture of hormones. Mix it with alcohol and you have a candidate for the ER. With testosterone all activities become a competition. Men will create a game out of any activity. With games come challenges and dares. With challenges and dares come pain and broken body parts and maybe a page in the Darwin awards. Most women do not have great levels of testosterone so they do not, nor ever will understand why men risk life and limb for a bet or a dare or for the fun of it. I mean, who would make up a game to see who could jump off a moving horse onto a bull with horns to wrestle the bull to the ground the fastest? Never get a bunch of guys, sitting around a table drinking beer, to make up a new game or challenge. Men have entered the woods, naked and unarmed just to see if they could survive. In today's competitions we try to follow rules to keep from killing each other while beating on each other. Making matters worse, testosterone is linked to success and failure. Men who are told they are great have higher levels of testosterone than men who are scolded for failure. High levels of testosterone are often cited for problems of sex-addiction.

Losing It

After the age of 30, testosterone levels decline about 1% a year. This might explain why some men start doing wilder and crazier things in their 40's, a mid-life crisis of sorts. They feel they are losing their edginess and thus are attempting to regain their fleeing manhood. It is not a bad thing and it does explain buying a motorcycle, taking up sky-diving or acting like a rock star while heading over the hill. How many times have we heard a woman tell a man to start acting his age? Well, truth be told, he is acting his age; his testicular age. Evidently there is no age limit for this behavior.

In the Beginning

To better understand the human male psyche we need to start at the beginning and follow him to manhood. A baby boy is born. He gasps and lets out a yell. Following that he poops. All done he reaches for the boob, gets his lips moving, latches on to the nipple and sucks.

A half hour later he is full, lets out a burp, passes gas and falls into a contended sleep. He is a happy boy. With a routine like that he would be a happy man. A few years later he discovers an appendage between his legs. He plays with it. He is a happy boy on his way to being a happy man.

A mother is giving her three year old son a bath. Holding his penis he asks his mom, "Is this my brain?" "No," she says, "Not yet".

Boys will be Boys

"Boys will be boys", is a very common saying in the US "What can you do?" and "What can you say?" rolls off the lips of mothers everywhere. Boys have the 'Y' chromosome with the prevailing 'guy' genes that go with it. Boys are not forgetful, they simply are not aware of what they are doing half of the time. Their neurons are not completely connected yet. They seem clueless, and that follows them all their lives. They are doing what comes naturally; butting heads, rolling on the ground, running in circles, chasing, and playing 'grab ass'. Boys appear hyper-active, but that is because the physical connector genes are preparing him for the rigors of manhood.

Manhood Rituals

Historically, boys around the ages of ten to twelve start their manhood training. Every society has different expectations of males, but no matter where you are, boys are expected to learn man stuff. The American Indians had several rites of passage from boyhood to manhood. Perhaps the most brutal rituals were found in the Mandan Indian tribe. Read what their young men went through; it is beyond excruciating. The Vikings, Greeks, Spartans, Mongols, and tribesmen around the world invented dangerous, and often painful, trials for young men. Then and today, training for battle was usually the first action a boy learned. Boys seem to naturally make weapons out of any stick or club they find. When I was a kid, we played tag shooting at each other with B B guns. We tried not to put anyone's eye out.

37

Puberty, Hair and Sticky Underwear

From birth through puberty, a male struggles through physical and emotional development. At puberty, his Y chromosome kicks in to high gear. Hormones are raging, and he is producing woodys/ stiffys 24/7. Pubic hair arrives, and voices are changing; body odor is apparent, and boys want to act like men but they are still living at home. Sex is on the mind of every teenage boy. Breasts make boys salivate. Slow dancing at the school dance insures sticky underwear. And yet, the mental neurons are falling behind the physical curve.

Life-time Reward

As it turns out, the desire to masturbate never abates. Stroking the ol' fire arm is just as much fun 50 years later as it was the first time. The drive to spill the seed comes from the pressure of constant production of sperm. An evolutionary advance to make sure the human male goes forth and multiplies. Having intercourse does not stem the tide completely. Part of masturbating is the fantasy fulfillment in the reward section of the brain. Rarely do men get to act out their sexual fantasies in real life, so stroking the rod while thinking about those fantasies sate those wishes. Women enjoy the activity also, but not nearly as often as men. Plus, women can usually get men to act out whatever fantasy they have.

Another classic joke that apparently only men know is the one about a mother catching her son masturbating. She says, "If you keep doing that you will go blind." He responds, "I will just do it until I need glasses." "What is a Yankee"? The same as a quickie, but a guy can do it himself.

Men Must be Men

Men meet together to ensure and enrich their manhood. Sure having sex with women helps stroke a man's genetic need to seed, but hanging with other men puts the man in manhood. With other men, a guy can be a guy. He can swear, fart, burp, drink, get sloppy, be gross, compete, and play games. Men do not want to hang around women who fart, burp, and get sloppy. Most men want to roar, and be stupid. Those are good times. Most men do not judge other men; that seems to be a woman's job. Most women do not understand the male need for 'male only' company. It is genetically wired that men find a group or groups of men who do 'guy' stuff.

Comfort Zone

Every man needs a comfort zone. It is a place where he is safe from criticism, safe from conflict, safe from women. It can be a room, a teepee, a gym, a hunting trip, fishing a river bank, even a garage. It is a place where he can have his 'stuff' like trophies, beer mugs, posters, football jerseys and non-female garb. Most importantly the furniture does not have to match.

Nerd Herd

Man groups are not just beer drinking, back slapping, penile Olympics and testosterone driven groups. They are herds of like-minded guys. 'Gamers,' 'skaters,' 'trekkies,' 'geeks,' 'nerds', poker players, or chess club guys are some examples of like-minded guys.

Layers of Brain

The picture of today's man should be getting clearer. We are getting closer to the answer of "What is a man"? We have been describing much of the criteria that need to be considered while trying to determine the make-up of a man. Looking at the evolution of the brain is important. Men have a series of brain overlays. The reptilian brain is covered with a mammalian fabric which is covered by a primate fabric which is covered by a human consciousness fabric. Testosterone has limited man's expression of safety. The male explores. The male takes chances. His multilayered brain slides up and down its evolutionary floors and sometimes acts impulsively. The male brain knows no bounds. It was important for the human race that men continuously tested the limits of survival. It was important that men did not over think their actions. Who in their right mind walks into blind caves, or treks through thick jungles, or sails the wild oceans in tiny ships or rafts? Men are willing to go anywhere, fight anything, and live off the wild land. He is both conscious and unconscious at the same time. Sometimes it seems this planet is not big enough for man.

Man Quiz

Are you a typical male, a guy, a Y chromosomal directed man? I have designed a man quiz. You will be able to see where you fit on the "Man Curve". It is a multiple answer quiz with a point score at the end for grading. Get a piece of paper to write down your answers before you tally your score. Do not mark on the quiz, you may want someone else to take the quiz but not see your answers.

1. You are making a peanut butter and jelly sandwich. You spread the peanut butter on one slice of bread.

   A. You clean the knife before putting it into the jelly.
   B. You put the knife with peanut butter on it into the jelly.
   C. You lick the knife clean then put it in the jelly.

2. You clean your bathroom because...

   A. You want your mother to be proud.
   B. After a few weeks it smells.
   C. You girlfriend will not shower with you if the tub is dirty.

3. You have a two day week-end golf tournament coming up. You missed the last one. You and your partner are signed up. Your wife tells you it is your grandson's birthday on Saturday and he is having a party.

   A. You tell your partner you cannot play.
   B. You whine to your wife but go grumpily to the party with a small present.
   C. You play the tournament, show up late to the party, but you bring a big gift.

4. You change the sheets on your bed…

   A. When your mom drops off of new sheets from a linen sale.
   B. When all the corners pull loose and you are lying on the mattress.
   C. Before your girlfriend comes over because she won't sleep with you on dirty sheets.

5. When you do your laundry (because you can't get anyone to do it for you)…

   A. You separate the whites from the colors, and pre-wash stains.
   B. All the clothes go in at once, and your whites will have a tint of blue or pink.
   C. It is the day after you run out of clean underwear.

6. Before you go out with your buddies you shower, shave, and sprinkle on cologne

   A. Because you want to impress your buddies.
   B. It just feels good.
   C. You hope to hook up and get laid.

7. You help your wife with the dishes because…

    A. You like to be helpful.
    B. She has scowled sufficiently.
    C. You hope to get laid.

8. You go to your neighbor's house for a beer with the gang, and you tell your wife you will be home by 10 PM.

    A. You leave the neighbor's house at 9:45 PM so you can be home by 10 PM.
    B. You get home at 11 PM and apologize to your wife for being late.
    C. You get home at 1 AM. After all, you are the one who has to get up and go to work so what's the big deal?

9. You take your wife to a dinner and a movie of her choice twice a month…

    A. Because you are kind and thoughtful.
    B. It pays to keep mama happy.
    C. You are hoping to have sex at least twice a month.

10. On Sunday you sleep late, don't shave, and you wear an old T-shirt all day because

    A. At least once a week you can let go.
    B. You are the man of the house.
    C. You just had sex last night and it's going to be another two weeks before it happens again.

To score this quiz, give 1 point for every 'A' answer, 2 points for every 'B' answer, and 3 points for every 'C' answer.

If you score 10 – 14, get a DNA test to make sure you have a 'Y' chromosome.

If you score 15 – 19, you are a 'girly' man.

If you score 20 – 24, celebrate your manhood.

If you score 25 – 30, you are 'Da Man'.

Man Jokes

Rarely do any jokes about men involve the use of brains.

They are about 'guts', endurance, and a tolerance for pain. There are a lot of sayings and one-liners and codes describing men. "Take it like a man," Be a "real man", "Man-up ", "Cowboy up", "A man's got to do what a man's got to do", and "the code of the West where a man is a man", are just a few of them. Throwing in something about testicles is also part of a man's description. He has the 'balls' or does not have the 'balls' to do it. 'Balls' translates into bravery or courage. Sometimes you meet a woman with 'balls'. (To paraphrase Betty White, she says balls are weak and sensitive. If you want to be tough, grow a vagina, it can take a constant beating.) All these sayings really mean a guy is about to do something stupid and he just can't help himself. Add in some alcohol and the dumb just becomes dumber.

Man Tombstones

Tombstone inscriptions in a man-only cemetery may read: "Now watch how a real man does it", "Yes, I know what I am doing", "Hey, trust me", "Don't worry, I have done this a million times", "What's the worst that can happen?", "That doesn't look so hard to do", and "A little shock never hurt nobody". We also have our own movies called "Dumb and Dumber" and "The Jackass" movies.

There are a lot of jokes about men and their characteristics. Guys do guy stuff. For a while there were some jokes going around called "Real Man" jokes. Q. How many men does it take to change a light bulb? A. None, real men are not afraid of the dark. Q. How many men does it take to screw in a light bulb? A. Three, one to screw in the bulb and two to listen to him brag about the screwing part. Q. How can you tell a real man when you see him? A. He is giggling on the way home from a vasectomy. Q. How many honest, intelligent, caring men does it take to do the dishes? A. Both of them. (This is a female joke about men.)

Helmet and Cup

Perhaps the following fact describes best the mental processes of the male brain. The first testicular guard (cup) was used in baseball and ice hockey in 1874. The first baseball helmet was used in 1934, for the NFL it was 1943. It only took 60 years in baseball to figure out the brain was important also. I also read that the helmet in ice hockey was not required until 1974 that is 100 years later for hockey players. It is a very sharp learning curve when a man gets hit in the 'nads'. Getting hit in the head is a manly thing; you just shake it off and go back in.

Man Jokes About Sex

For 350 million years the biological imperative for the male was to spread his seed in every fertile field he could find. When it comes to sex, nothing is too weird or too funny for men.

Q. How can you tell if a man is aroused? A. He is breathing.

Q. Why do men like love at first sight? A. It saves them a lot of time.

Q. Why were men given larger brains than dogs? A. So they wouldn't' hump women's legs at cocktail parties.

Don't worry; it only seems kinky the first time.

Man and Beer

The oldest known written recipe in the world is for beer

The oldest known code of laws is the Hammurabi from ancient Babylonia, about 1750 BCE. It called for the death penalty for bartenders guilty of watering down their beer.

The first brewery in America was built in Hoboken, NJ, in 1642.

"Utshwala" is Zulu for beer.

Tossing salted peanuts in a glass of beer makes the peanuts dance.

It is estimated that a pint of beer is lifted 10 times before it is gone. A 16 ounce beer would give you a 10 pound workout.

Collecting beer coasters is called Tegestology.

Q. How does a man plan for the future? A. He buys 2 cases of beer instead of one.

Q. What is a man's 7 course dinner? A. A hot dog and a six pack.

Q. What is the best way to break down a man? A. Have him choose between a naked woman and a six pack of beer.

Reasons Men Prefer Rifles to Women

1. You can trade in an old 44 for a new 22. 2. You can keep one rifle at home and have another one for the road. 3. If you admire a friend's rifle he will probably let you try it out. 4. Your rifle will stay with you even if you run out of ammo. 5. A rifle does not mind if you go to sleep after you use it.

A Guy Fairy Tale

Once upon a time, a prince asked a beautiful princess to marry him. She said, "No". And the prince lived happily ever after and rode motorcycles and went fishing and hunting and played golf and dated women half his age and drank beer and Scotch and had tons of money and left the toilet seat up and farted whenever he wanted.

Why Men are Happier than Women

Your last name always stays the same. The garage is yours. Wedding plans take care of themselves. Chocolate is just another snack. You can never be pregnant. You can wear a white T-shirt to a water park. You can wear NO shirt to a water park. The world is your urinal. Same work, more pay. Wrinkles add character. Wedding dress $5000, tux rental $100. People never stare at your chest when you are talking to them. One mood at a time. You know stuff about tanks. A five day vacation requires only one small suitcase. You can open all your own jars. You get extra credit for the slightest act of thoughtfulness. If someone forgets to invite you somewhere, he or she can still be your friend. Man's underwear is $8.95 for a three-pack. Three pairs of shoes are more than enough. You never have strap problems in public. You are unable to see wrinkles in your clothes. The same hair style lasts for years. You can play with toys all your life. You can choose to grow a mustache. Nick names for your buddies are "Fat Boy", "Dickhead", and "Shit for Brains". A man has 6 items in his bathroom; a woman has 337. You may see another guy at a party wearing the same thing you have on and you might get to be friends for life.

Conversations with a Man

A shrug, a shoulder slump, a grunt, upturned hands, and a smirk are all perfectly good forms of male conversation. "Dude" can be said with a dozen different inflections meaning a dozen different things. "Yo" or "Yo Mama" are perfectly good ways to say "Hi," or answer a question. Grunting is a perfectly good response to most questions or statements. "Oh Man," is another phrase with multiple meanings depending on inflection. If a guy ends a sentence with the word "Man" then some anger is implied. When a guy says, "Fucks up man?" the other guys know he is emotionally upset with current conditions, and wants to know what's going on. If he just says, "Fucks up?" then he is inquiring about current events.

Sports Talk

Complementing a buddy, while playing sports, involves one word sentences. In golf for instance, if your buddy makes a good read of the green and sinks a twenty foot putt, you simply say, "Putt," the rest of the compliment is implied and understood. A good, long, straight drive is "Drive," the rest is understood. Shooting pool might involve the words "Shot" or "Bank". In baseball it might call for "Hit" or "Throw". All else is understood. Women are totally confused by one word sentences.

While having a beer a guy might say to his buddy, "Wife's pissed". There is an entire paragraph of meaning in those two words. His buddy might say, "Happens," or "Women!" or even just a knowing head shake. The rest is understood. Then they have another beer and watch the game. Another conversation might go like this, "Bill's getting married." A typical response might be, "Fucks he thinkin?" or "No shit" or "Damn" or even a shrug, and the rest is understood. Men don't have to explain themselves to each other. Meanings are understood. Men have no need for personal pronouns; verbs and direct objects are usually enough. It is amazing how guys understand each other easily but women seem to have a terrible time conversing with a man.

None of this is to imply that men are idiots or non-literates. Men are intelligent in numerous ways. Men can be great authors, writers, poets and literary agents. But, when men communicate with each other in a non-written form, gestures, sounds, and body language are easily understood. Much of what is not said is understood. Long explanations are not necessary. Too many details spoil the story unless it is about having sex with identical twins. Be wary of men who talk too much, they are probably salesmen or politicians.

The Y Chromosome

Men are pretty much what they seem to be. What you see is what you get. Men do not change as they get older. They get more like themselves. That is to say they get less like women. The Y chromosome is evolving. It has changed more than any other chromosome in the human body. It has lost hundreds of genes and is now down to about 80. Even so, male behavior does not seem to have changed over the past 35,000 years. The frontal cortex is dueling with the primitive reptilian brain. Life can be confusing for men, but that never stopped them from plowing ahead.

Summary

Defining a man involves a lot of criteria. He is hard wired for many behaviors. He forms bonds with men and women. Often his family is his pride. A man is male/guy, a brother, father, son, husband, partner, lover, trainer, leader, teacher, and a builder. He is a loyal friend and a protector. He is not to cry or whine. His brain has evolved with a frontal cortex that enables emotions, ideals, conscience, and motivation. Overlaying this boy-to-man cycle is his cultural and environmental influences. Learning to be a man has many different meanings in different cultures/cities/countries. Most men are doing the best they can. He is what he is. He can be as good as it gets or as bad as it gets. Most men do respond positively to strokes and hugs. Let the man be the man (unless he is sick, then baby him).

Chapter 10

What is a Woman?

Some people would call me crazy for writing a chapter defining women. I agree women are possibly the most difficult of entities to define. Women claim the shortest book ever written is, "What Men Know About Women." And the longest book is "What Men Think They Know About women."

I cannot reveal the secret to understanding women; there are too many coded, secret, complex, variable, unknown mysteries involved. What I will do is offer some known chemical and genetic facts and some observations of female behavior that have occurred over the past billion years. Those historical facts and behaviors impact the female behavior of today. And while the human female exhibits all of the historical behaviors of the past, they have added some new angles that confuse, or influence (depending on your perspective) the behaviors of women today. Betty *has* to be a child, an adult, a sex partner, a baby factory, a care giver, and eventually a menopause client. Some say it is not easy to be a woman.

There are a lot of criteria to consider when describing women. And a woman's opinion of women will be different from a man's opinion of women. Men, being more simple than women, have simple criteria for evaluating them. Women, being so more highly evolved than men, have a complex matrix of score keeping.

Not Manic

This chapter will not be as manic as the chapter on men. Women do not have a penis they can wave around in the air like some sort of magic wand. However, they do have breasts and a vagina which may provide years of entertainment, adventure, and excitement. They do not, as a habit, risk life and limb on a bet. They do travel on a roller coaster of emotions and men could risk permanent damage if they snicker at the wrong time.

Scientific Description

A woman is a member of Homo sapiens with a genome that includes two X chromosomes. There is no Y chromosome. She is a vertebrate/mammal/primate/hominid with an opposable thumb. Women produce a reproductive cell called an egg. Women have babies. A male cannot naturally have offspring. A woman is the end product of billions of years of evolutionary female genetic rules.

X chromosome

The X chromosome really defines the woman. The X chromosome is the giver of life. An organism can survive and grow and mature with only one X chromosome. An organism with only a Y chromosome will die. Women have two X chromosomes. One X gives life and the other X tells you how hard it was. The Y chromosome is thought to have fragmented off an X chromosome, but apparently did not get the genes necessary for life. Early life was only female. The default sex is female. All embryos start out as female, but eventually a Y chromosome will kick in hormonal commands and a male begins to develop. Males have a very limited role in reproduction and gestation. The queen bee is a great example of the power of the female. She swarms with a dozen males, collects their sperm, and then holds it for life dispensing the sperm whenever it is necessary to fertilize a few eggs (the males die after the sperm is happily given). The queen has complete control over the future outcome of the egg. She gives meaning to the phrase 'queen mother'. The woman with two X's has the genes that make her special. She is the mother and the nurturer. Without her, there is no offspring, no reproduction, and no humans.

Growing up Female

Since I did not grow up female, I have had several women read this chapter for comment. Many of their comments are included in this chapter, along with my observations as an affected by-stander.

Puberty and Stuffed Bras

Just as in the chapter on men, in order to understand the female psyche we need to start at the beginning, and follow her through womanhood. The first decade for women may be about being a little girl, having tea parties, and maybe being a princess; then, boom, puberty hits. Puberty can be difficult for girls. Whereas boys are excited about getting pubic hair and a larger penis, girls are more sensitive and less secure about their body image. Girls seem to be divided into three groups concerning the onset of puberty. One group is excited about becoming women and embraces the coming changes. Another group is the "it-is-what-it-is no-getting-out-of-it" group. The third group is explained by the comment, "Oh crap". Between the ages of 8 and 14 these changes start to take place. Hormones kick off the change in growth, skin problems and personal sensitivity. The process may take 2 to 3 years. Each decade, puberty seems to jump the gun earlier and earlier. I remember hearing mothers blaming the hormones in dairy milk for the early arrival of breasts on young girls.

Early Womanhood rituals

Pubescent girls have tough emotional challenges. Wearing a bra seems to be one and a vexation of sorts for girls. Many young girls wish to have some definite 'chest bumps' by 7th grade to fit in. Stuffing tissue into those 'A' or 'B' cups was a common practice. Make-up, ear rings, two piece bathing suits, shaving, and matching pants and tops all come screaming at the teen-age girl during puberty (so I have been told).

Princess Classes

In London, classes on how to be a princess are being offered. It is a one day class followed by a series of weeklong summer camps for 8 to 11 year old girls. For only $4,000 young girls can learn about historic and modern princesses, along with proper etiquette for social settings. Instruction includes: how to curtsy, attendance at a mock tea party, how to smooth out your dress while sitting, stirring a cup of tea and receiving compliments. The goal is to instill self-control and confidence.

(48% of American workers say they work with a "workplace Princess" defined as a coworker with a sense of entitlement or privilege. 16% of those surveyed said their work-place princess was a man.)

Aunt Flo

The biggest life changing event in any woman's life is menstruation. Whether a woman wants a baby or not, she must, on a monthly basis, prepare for one. Menstruation comes with many nicknames. As found on the internet, a few are: Period, The Curse, Aunt Flo, Aunt Rose, My Friend, Leak Week, Red River Valley, The Shinning, and TOTM (time of the month).

Cycles

A woman would like to be defined by her personality and brain, her feelings and strengths. Because the female mammal must prepare her body for pregnancy she must go through a reproductions cycle and that may over-ride her normal behavior. A lot of hormones, pheromones and neuropeptides are involved in this process. On average, women ovulate every 28 days. Her sensitivity and sexual drives will vary from day to day depending on hormonal ebb and flow. Adult women who are ovulating are more inclined to 'mate' than not. One Study in 'Health Day', 2012 suggests that women who are ovulating buy sexier clothes, and are more forgiving of a man's manners and hygiene. Ovulating involves surges of estrogen that cause more sensitive nipples and a swelling of the clitoris. The changes in hormone flow, cause huge surges, creating a sex drive of curiosity, and desire. Many women suddenly have a 'tingling' feeling when near a hunky, pheromone dripping, male.

One study from the UK says that birth control pills suppress women's interest in "masculine" men, making "boyish" men more attractive. The theory holds that women prefer the big/hunky/alpha male/rugged type (good sperm) during ovulation, but when this is blocked (as when taking the pill) they prefer softer, more caring man. It would do for men to know what day it is during that pill taking routine. (One woman told me her husband charted her cycle so he could empathize with her feelings ....ultra-sweet or what?)

Period Myths

Also found on the internet are common myths about TOTM. Do not go swimming in the ocean; your period scent might attract sharks. Your pad/tampon will swell up with water, get too heavy, and you might drown. Another is that a teen using a tampon will lose her virginity. What is not a myth is PMS. Pre-menstrual problems are very real for many women. When the period fairy drops in cramping, bloating, acne, mood swings and tender breasts can be a result.

480 Seriously?

If a woman starts her period at age 13, and it goes until age 53, that is 40 years of visits by the period fairy. At 12 times a year, that is 480 interruptions of daily life. That is 480 reminders that a woman is not in control of her body. That is nature intervening, with 480 opportunities for bloating, hormone surges, cramps, stained clothes and strapping on a pad. If the average period lasts 5 days, that's 2400 days, 200 months, 6.58 years rafting the red river in a life-time. According to one "Healthy Living" internet page, a woman's period, over a life-time, costs about $18,000. Another website, called "vagina maintenance", estimates that in your 20s alone, vagina maintenance runs over $26,000. (The internet constantly amazes me at what can be found on any subject.) Following number 480 comes menopause, which is another bad trip. Not only is a woman at the mercy of nature, but men, religion, and ignorant myths intervene as well. I ask you, if you could come back for another life would you chose to come back as a man or a woman?

Period Poetry

Not to belabor the puberty/menstruation event but you can search the internet for menstruation poetry. Yes, poetry, a little weird, but who woulda-thunk it? There is even a web site for embarrassing menstruation stories. In decades past all this 'female stuff' was kind of hush-hush, today social media has brought forth anything and everything you can imagine regarding 'female stuff'. The *"Vagina Monologues",* is an excellent play in which woman's issues are discussed openly.

Ignorant Men

Men are quite ignorant about menstruation. There is no way a man can walk a mile in a woman's high heeled shoes. Interestingly enough, that has not kept them from making declarations and rules about the process. According to men of the past, menstruation seems to have magical powers. In ancient Rome, Pliny the Elder wrote that a menstruating woman who uncovers herself can scare away hailstorms. He also wrote that if she walks around the fields, caterpillars, worms and beetles will fall off the corn. (Pesticide companies could hire a few thousand women in Iowa to walk the corn fields, then have no need to spray the corn crop with pesticides, talk about 'organic') The Jewish Talmud claims menstruating women are unclean. ('The Red Tent' is an interesting read.) Women will contaminate anything they touch. Having sex with her husband when 'Aunt Flo' is visiting can be cause for arrest, even death, for the menstruating woman (tough love in this case).

In India a menstruating woman cannot cook food. If she touches a pickle it will rot ....that is some kind of magic! In some tribes the women must leave the village or live in a cowshed.

Synchronicity

An interesting hormonal effect that occurs when a group of women work or live together is that the timing of their periods may eventually coincide with one another. (One primitive myth is that if women's periods are not synchronized the universe might descend into chaos, I'm thinking just the opposite.)

Pity the unknowing male boss entering a room full of female workers during TOTM and wondering what was going on. Not that all women are erratic during their periods but with hot flashes, hormone surges, etc., the business office could seem a bit out of focus. Or picture the looks on the men's faces when an entire village of women are in synchrony and all leave for a week, leaving the men to clean, care for the kids, and cook. I am pretty sure the rules of leaving the village for menstruating women would change very quickly.

An Issue Over a Tissue

A man wants to be a woman's first love. A woman wants to be a man's last love. Once again, ignorance raises its ugly head. Virginity seems to be a super big deal for many men. They place an ungodly emphasis on virginity. In many countries around the world men will insist that doctors conduct virginity tests on girls. Put 'Virginity Tests' in your internet search bar and several pages of articles pop up. One, from October 2016, has an Egyptian lawmaker saying women should prove they are virgins in order to go to college. There are thousands of "honor" killings of young girls who do not pass the test. Searching for a hymen can be very elusive. Some men think taking a virgin brings good luck and can cure disease. (You just cannot stamp out ignorance.) On the other hand, it may be important to know that a woman can get hymen reconstruction surgery.

The Emerging Woman

Girls coming into adulthood have several choices to make. In many cultures, a woman has few choices available, but in western cultures like the US, she is only limited by her imagination. Career, college, marriage, children, freedom and self-discovery are just a few of the mental/social opportunities/hazards of womanhood. Modern Betty can explore space, run a business, go into medicine, seek adventure, or stay single. Physically, the emerging woman is ready for motherhood, but mentally she may want more development, more fine tuning. There is a battle between the genetic commands and the desire for social fulfillment. Sex becomes a major part of life at this time. Dealing with men becomes a major part of life at this time. Solidifying a style becomes a major part of life at this time.

Girls Gone Wild

Some women want to experience choices before settling down with a partner. More and more, women are enjoying their sexual freedom. Early twenties is the time for skinny dipping and perhaps flashing boobs for beads in New Orleans. One lady friend told me she was an equal opportunity woman and, asked men to flash their "package" for beads. Having friends with benefits (FWB), a new hybrid of having sex with friends without commitment, is common. (A study in 2015 found 2/3 of college students experienced "friends with benefits.")

Breasts

Men seem to be obsessed by women's breasts. Perhaps it is the nurturing aspect of breasts that appeals to men. More likely it is an erotic aspect that stimulates a quivering in a man's loins that makes breasts appeal to men. Men have probably created more slang words for a woman's breast than any other object on earth. Boobs, jugs, mamas, tits, balloons, bosom, busts, bazooms, dugs, sweater kittens, puppies, knockers, assets, melons, head lights, rack, ta-tas, fried eggs, and, for the poets, lactation station, are a few slang words for mammary glands. (Even women call them 'the girls'.) According to one survey, 32% of women consider their breasts to be their best feature. Some women are proud to be small breasted. As one woman told me, "Anything more than a handful or mouthful is wasted anyway".

Breast augmentation has made many doctors very rich, and has become common place. A story in the Arizona Republic reported that in 2015, of the 1.7 million cosmetic surgeries performed, breast augmentation accounted for 279,143 procedures. Additionally, 40,650 breast reductions were performed.

Uterus

A female/woman has a uniquely, special organ for the development of an embryo, the baby. It is called a uterus. The outer opening to the uterus is called a vagina. The vagina is actively sought out by the male. Much to the delight of the male, it contains muscles that can be and have been trained. Situated above the vagina, much to the delight of most women, is a feature called a clitoris. The clitoris is made of erectile tissue. It works like a penis, when excited it rises. Not like a 'Mr. Woody' but still a small volcano-like erection. The clitoris is loaded with neural sensors connected to the pleasure center in the brain. When done correctly, intercourse becomes a mutual delight for both men and women.

I saw a woman wearing a t-shirt that said, "I have the pussy, I make the rules."

Masturbation

Since the clitoris is erectile tissue, similar to that of men, it can be excited. When wired correctly the clitoris is a source of pleasure for many women when rubbed correctly. Women's fantasies tend to be more emotional and romantic than men's. Romance paperbacks for women are a multi-million dollar market. Some studies suggest that masturbation in women can also ease pain. Evidently the neurons connecting to the brain for pleasure, override those neurons that send pain to the brain. Betty may be thinking masturbation is better than suffering or taking drugs when in pain.

Genital Fashion Consciousness

Women seem to have an evolved fashion sense. Balance and composition are important to women. It seems it even carries over to things sexual. In July, 2015, a survey involving 105 women in Switzerland asked what women look for in a penis. Women ages 16 to 45 were shown a variety of pictures of male genitalia, and were asked which ones they found most attractive. (Probably not a show going prime time in the US.) Number one was overall cosmetic appearance. Second was the appearance of pubic hair. Tied for third was girth and appearance of the skin, and finally, shape of the tip. Apparently 'fashion' was more important than size. However, in another survey of 41 women, girth was considered most important when considering a one night stand. A lady friend pointed out to me that the first sexual encounter with a new man is a little tense. While a guy can see a woman's shape and size and have a pretty good idea of what he is getting, the woman has no idea what the man's 'package' is like; apparently size does matter.

Grooming Down Under (Not talking about Australia.)

Pubic area fashion has no boundaries. Heart-shaped, landing pad, big V, nude/shaved, and more are a few fashion patterns available for the female pubic patch. For the adventurous woman, pubic hair dyes are popular, pink for Valentine's Day for instance. I have been asked a few times, as a man, what pubic fashions do men like in women? Interestingly enough, that has never come up in casual conversation; I think most men are just happy to be in that neighborhood. Personally, I would say, "Bikini cut".

A Head of Hair

Apparently nothing says, "look at me", more than hair. A bad haircut can put a woman in tears. If a woman's hair is not 'behaving' it can be traumatizing. According to a newspaper article describing a poll of over 1000 women conducted by the magazine "Shop Smart" a fourth of women have cried after getting a haircut; a third have regretted a style change. After a dramatic event, like a break-up or job loss, half of the women color their hair and many have drastically changed the style of their hair. I do not know any men that radically change their hair color after a dramatic event; usually, they just drink.

Communication with a Woman

Joke of the year: Two women were quietly sitting together minding their own business.

Communication is the act of exchanging information or opinions. Women are very good at both sending and receiving subtle non-verbal signals; men not so much. Women can also read non-verbal signals very well; men not so much. Women are also great at reading hidden meanings or underlying currents in conversations; again, men not so much. We can see that females are genetically endowed with keen sensory perceptive skills.

30,000 – 15,000

Women, on average, use about 30,000 words a day. Men use, on average, only 15,000 words a day. Women will tell you they use twice as many words as men because they have to repeat everything they say to a man because men do not listen the first time.

Healthy Talk

Since conversation styles between men and women are so different the reason must be genetic. Visit anyone of a number of 'woman's health' blogs and you will see a common message is to talk. Talk to friends, talk to strangers, talk to a rock, whatever. Talking relieves stress, produces happy hormones, and leads to good health. Becoming close to a girlfriend increases the levels of progesterone, thus helping to boost mood and alleviate stress. Talking is therapy for women. (In my experience, women must be the healthiest people on earth.) Sometimes a "Bitch Fest" is necessary in order to 'vent'. It appears there is a hormonal basis for social bonding. The beauty salon is like a health spa for women. On any given day there is enough progesterone floating around the room to sedate a dozen men.

Don't You Remember?

When a guy forgets what his wife said a dialogue something like this took place: "Don't you remember honey? We were in the meat department at the store, I was on the phone with my mother and she had asked if we were coming over and I said no, then a girl from work who was pregnant walked by and I introduced you and she said she didn't know the sex of the baby and that was when I told you the Smiths were coming over for dinner and you had to get the extra chairs from the garage tonight". What he heard: "No sex tonight".

Secrets

From the DailyMail.com, 2009, a study of 3000 women indicated that the typical length of time a woman can keep a secret is 47 hours and 15 minutes. With men, they only remember what is said half the time so keeping a secret is easy.

Women will sometimes admit making a mistake. The last man who admitted he was wrong was General George Custer.

Female Detection System

Females had to develop sensory tools for picking the best male. They needed the strong male for protection and the healthy sperm for the offspring. Through evolution (trial and error) the females who instinctively (i.e. genetically) selected the right male had offspring that survived. Those female offspring had the right genetic make-up to continue to select the right male. Men will never know what that genetic selection process entails.

A woman comes screaming into the driveway, jumps out of the car, bursts into the house and yells to her husband, "I just won a million dollars in the lottery! Pack your bags." "Wow," he says, "Do I pack for the mountains or the beach?" "Doesn't matter" she says, "Just pack your bags and get out."

Betty's turmoil

When Betty goes out with her girlfriends she takes two Bettys with her: modern Betty (with an active frontal lobe) and ancient Betty. If she sees a big hunky, 'bad boy' type guy with thick hair and a non-compliant attitude, both Bettys react. Ancient Betty sees good sperm and a protector. Modern Betty is also attracted, but she wonders if he has a job, and maybe some money in the bank. Ancient Betty may go for a one night stand, or a fling lasting one mating season, or until distracted by the next 'hunky' bad boy. A cursory look at many relationships today shows ancient Betty is often in charge. Modern Betty may have sex but she carries a condom, evaluates long term chances, and waits for compatibility. Her frontal cortex is evolving and getting a good blood supply. Ultra-modern Betty skips the male drama and goes to the sperm bank for designer genes. Mature Betty wants to see a 401K and the lipid panel results.

Biological Drive

Betty hears her biological clock ticking. All her friends seem to be having babies. Her mom keeps asking for grandkids. She is now married, so it is time to get those eggs fertilized. One important result of pregnancy and raising offspring is a hormonal suppression of self interest in order to promote the well-being of another. Carrying an embryo for 9 months, then caring for a screaming little thing, takes more than just a warm fuzzy feeling. This hormonal suppression may be the definition of motherhood. Self-sacrifice and motherhood seem to go together. "Mother earth", "mother nature," "mother may I," and a hundred other references to 'mother' are found throughout human history.

Mommy Brain

In evolution, traits do not become helpful because there is a need. Helpful traits persist because those genes are successfully transferred to surviving offspring. Mothers that responded to the 'cry' of the offspring aided in the survival of the offspring, therefore the genes of 'helpful mommy' swam in the gene pool of life. The mommy brain fed the kids, protected the kids, and patiently raised the kids at the sacrifice of her well-being. Mom's protection is legendary throughout the animal kingdom. (To his credit, today's male is becoming more involved with child care.)

John West

Carry Over of Compassion

Fortunately for the scheme of life, this hormonal suppression of self-interest floated through all phases of female behavior. Females became more emotional, more caring, and more compassionate in their daily life. This promoted social integration. Females grouped together and thrived together. Females had to survive for the sake of the offspring. Females learned to form bonds, social units and began the foundation for civilization.

A Man Never Knows

She was in the kitchen preparing to boil eggs for breakfast. He walked in. She turned and said, "You've got to make love to me this very moment." His eyes lit up and he thought, "This is my lucky day." Not wanting to lose the moment took her right there on the kitchen table. Afterwards she said, "Thanks" and returned to the stove. Puzzled he asked, "What was that about?" She explained, "The egg timer is broken."

Advice to Men

There are no known rules for a woman's sexual behavior. Something in their genetic, sensory, cortex turns them on or off. If we look back through nature and examine female behavior, a few tips are seen. Females are looking for a healthy sperm donor, maybe with an appropriate shelter. Men need to look good. Good grooming, nicely ironed clothes, good hygiene and a clean, neat crib will go a long way as positive stimuli for a woman. I overheard a woman talking to her girlfriend, complaining about a guy who wanted her to spend the night with him. She said the guy's bathroom was dirty, and no way was she going to take a shower in that guy's place. From then on I always cleaned my bathroom when I was inviting a woman to my place.

When asked what canine qualities women would like to see in a man, the top answer was "In perennial good mood." Two-thirds of the respondents said they would not date anyone who did not like their dog. The lesson here is to always have some doggie treats in your pocket.

Women's Jokes about Sex

He: Since I first laid eyes on you, I've wanted to make love to you in the worst way.

A. She: You succeeded.

Q. How do you know if a man is dead? A. The sex is the same but there is less ironing.

Q. What is a man's idea of foreplay? A. Brace yourself sweetie.

Women are evolving mentally and culturally, often at odds with their biological imperative. As men say, "You can't live with them and you can't live without them" or is that what women say about men?

One More Concept

After reading chapters 9 and 10 we can take away an essential concept. Men need to hang out with other men to do man stuff. Women need to hang out with other women to do women stuff. Give your partner time to hang with their 'friends' and life together will be happy.

Chapter 11

What is Love?

Profound Questions

Before we go to "Finding a Mate" (chapter 12) we need to define 'Love.' Betty wants to know how she will know if she is in love. She wants to know if her love will last and if her love is true. These are questions she and all women ask. Is there any dumber answer than, "When it is right, you will know it'" or "Love will find you when you least expect it"? (I least expect to find love at 3:00 am when I am sleeping and so far I am right.) Even the Bobs of the world have questions about love. Love can be quite confusing but quite useful when selecting a mate. Once we know what love is, then we can recognize it, know how it feels and then know if we are in it.

What is Love?

"To be in love is merely to be in a state of perceptual anesthesia."

– H.L. Mencken

"Love is the master key that opens the gates of happiness."

– Oliver Wendell Holmes

"Love is the irresistible desire to be irresistibly desired."

– Mark Twain

"Love is the only sane and satisfactory answer to the problem of human existence."

– Erich Fromm

"If you would be loved, love and be lovable."

– Benjamin Franklin (1755)

And from the very insightful woman Marguerite Duras (a French writer and movie director, 1914-1996) "You have to be very fond of men. Very, very fond. You have to be very fond of them to love them. Otherwise they are simply unbearable."

More Love

At first blush, defining love may seem like an unanswerable task. Whole books have been written about love, its forms, meanings, and often times, its consequences. As you can see from some of the quotes above there are as many ideas of love as there are people. A short list of some types of love include: parental love, brotherly love, aesthetic love, love of sport, love of country, and the focus of this book, romantic love. The word 'love' gets thrown around like stares at a nude beach. Some descriptions of love include: frustrating, fleeting, exhilarating, euphoric, heart wrenching, spicy, hot, enchanting, and even painful.

Love can be used as a noun, as in, "love makes the world go around," a verb, as in, "Betty loves Bob," an adjective, as in, "that is a lovely sunset," as an adverb, as in, 'she talks lovingly to her baby,' and other parts of speech. For fun, decide how 'love' is used (part of speech) in the following sentences. "I would love to jump her bones." "We made love all night." "I put a little love in every cookie I bake."

A scientist might define love as a chemical imbalance or a chemical neural event in the brain brought on by several factors. However, not all chemical imbalances are love; rage comes to mind. The word generally used for those chemical imbalances is emotion. Love is an emotion, one of a vast array of emotions the human is capable of feeling.

Emotions

The human brain is a wonderful and curious organ. It is loaded with millions of receptors that trigger emotions. Emotions are set off by conscious and unconscious triggers. Someone cutting you off in traffic, or being rude, or bumping into you on purpose will elicit conscious emotional triggers. It is the unconscious triggers that are confusing. Often times we do not know why we feel the way we do. Feelings of love and attraction are two of those unconscious events.

Type the word 'emotions' on an internet search and a variety of lists will pop up. We are looking for the 'good' feeling ones. One list would include: pleased, wonderful, elated, hopeful, inspired, happy, eager, joy, optimism, awe, ecstasy, and of course love. All things considered, we see that 'love' is not a single feeling, but a complex network of feelings that form the 'love' emotion. It is like a rope spun of many fibers. Some of those positive fibers include: desire, respect, admiration, empathy, pride, wonderment, happiness and peace.

But that is not all. The human body is a neural-electronic-chemical machine. Feelings will elicit a physiological response all over the body. A survey I read asked 700 people to describe where emotions were felt in the body. The answers were the same across sex and cultures. A short summary showed 'happiness' was felt head to toe, in the arms and legs with the most feeling in the heart. Love was felt in the head, arms, and chest to loins, with the most felt in the head, heart, and loins. Pride was felt most in the head and heart. There are physical manifestations of feelings and emotions that must be included in our discussion of love.

Euphoria

Euphoria is defined as an irrational feeling of happiness. This feeling is centered in the brain. I call that part of the brain the 'happy place'. A number of hormones in the body can affect the 'happy place.' Our genes determine when, where, how much, or how many hormones may be released.

Am I in Love?

You see Bob or Betty for the first time. Your eyes meet, you feel your heart beating faster, you touch hands, and the electric shock speeds through your body. You breathe in her/his sweet smell, your knees may get weak, you feel warm all over, and your loins feel a definite stirring. Your genetic markers have heightened your senses and stimulated your physiological processes and you become light headed. Sensory directives kick up your chemistry, and your body experiences elevated levels of the neurotransmitter norepinephrine. This in turn can make you jittery, thus clumsy, and a little out of sync. That can be followed by elevated levels of dopamine. Dopamine causes all sorts of stimulations to the brain. You might become fidgety with extra energy. You begin to notice slight details about the other person you had not noticed before. Everything seems special and unique. The room may seem brighter because your pupils will dilate when seeing a person who sparks your interest. Falling in love initially makes you more mellow than usual, and you find yourself quite agreeable in an attempt to merge with your new interest. You might even feel like you have known this person for a long time. Have you ever caught yourself saying, "I feel like I have known you forever," to someone you just met? Experiencing a feeling of familiarity is a sure sign of chemistry at work and one part of the love puzzle drops in place. One of the dumbest definitions of love I have ever heard is, "Love is never having to say you're sorry." Who makes that crap up? Being in love does not mean you can do nothing wrong.

Sex

One of the best stimulants for 'happy juice' production is physical groping and sex organ massaging. Having intercourse stimulates a meteoric feeling in the reward center. This may come as no surprise, but for men (and I mean about 90% of men) romance includes sex. The evening may be formal, or casual or anywhere in between, but at the end of the night most men hope sex is involved. Most women do not need sex at the end of the night. Plus, women usually know, hours ahead of time, if sex is going to happen. For many men, sex is the climax of the evening, whereas for women the high point of the evening is the conversation and foreplay. Men express feelings with action. Women express feelings in words.

Definition of Love

Love is not a single thing. It begins as a complex, somewhat impossible combination of chance alignments of unconscious perceptions. The chemistry, vibe, and visual stimulation create emotions that radiate out and form a charged cloud of emotions. We lose control of our emotions and actions even when we think we are in charge. Love is a tapestry of chemical, neural, and electrical, and genetic fibers interwoven with an euphoric thunderstorm outcome.

For two people to fall in love it takes, at the outset, a mutual, sympathetic, harmonious genetic code from both people. With time, feelings grow. Neural connections form in the brain and join with penal or vaginal stimulations for a strong affectionate feeling. You may be falling in love when a caring feeling for your partner outweighs the lusty feeling of sex. This takes time, it takes encoding in the frontal cortex. You cannot rush love.

Will My Love Last?

A woman's attitude toward sex goes a long way toward enticing a man for a long-term relationship (the reverse is also true). Eventually, a woman has to get a man's thoughts off sex and on to the world of feelings and commitment. Men need to get past the lusty feelings to get to the loving feeling; that takes time. As mentioned, sexual cravings and the desire to reproduce are genetically ingrained in living things. Too many marriages occur after two or three months with the feeling that this sexual euphoria will never stop. Wanting sex is okay but to get to the next level, lasting love, requires feelings of friendship and loyalty. Lasting love is an emotion that needs conscious mental involvement along with the unconscious genetic push. Using the analogy of multiple fibers interwoven together to make a strong rope, the more emotional fibers interwoven together the stronger, and therefore more lasting, the love. Having more things in common insures a greater 'network' of feelings. If the attraction is only a single thread of desire, or one of admiration, then the bond is easily broken. I suggest a rule of 'TEN'. That is, Betty should count up the things she loves about Bob, and how he makes her feel, and if she gets to ten then there is hope for a lasting love. Of course, Bob must also count up the things he loves about Betty and hope there are ten. The cool thing is they do not have to be the same ten things.

Time is the Test

You know your love will stand the test of time if all the sensory, conscious and unconscious triggers are still firing after one year. Marriage may enter the picture if life goals are in sync. Know that being in love may not mean that marriage is the next step. (Know also that loving someone and being in love with someone is not the same thing.)

Now you know what love is, and you have a formula to test its 'trueness'. You should be able to recognize feelings that lead to happiness and euphoria. All emotions originate in the brain and are chemically induced. The crazy thing is, you can feel the effects of love-induced chemicals throughout your body, in your heart, knees, chest, cramps in your toes, and of course in your loins. How you use this 'love' feeling to select a mate is in the next chapter. We will see why Betty is attracted to Bob, and Bob to Betty.

One final warning; more than one person can stimulate those emotional fibers at the same time.

Chapter 12

Finding a Mate

There is a joke going around the internet I have seen several times with slightly different wording but with the same message. It illustrates the common perception of the difference between how women and men look for a prospective spouse.

Husband Store

A store that sells new husbands has opened up in New York City where a woman may go to choose a husband. Among the instructions at the entrance of the store is a description of how the store operates. The sign says: You may visit the store ONLY ONCE! There are six floors and the value of the products increases as the shopper ascends the flights. The shopper may choose any item from a particular floor or may choose to go up to the next floor. Once you go up to the next floor you MAY NOT go back. So, a woman goes to the husband store to find a husband.

Floor 1 – The sign says: These men have jobs. She looks in the door but decides to go on.

Floor 2 – The sign says: These men have jobs and love kids. That's nice she thinks but I want more so she goes   to   the next floor.

Floor 3 – The sign says: These men have jobs, love kids, and are extremely good looking. She looks in the door and sure enough the guys are looking good. But she knows there are three more floors, and this could get a lot better, so up she goes.

Floor 4 – The sign says: These men have jobs, love kids, are 'Drop Dead' gorgeous and help with housework.
Somehow this is not enough, and she heads up one more floor.

Floor 5 – The sign says: These men have jobs, love kids, are drop dead gorgeous, help with Housework, and have a strong romantic streak. She is very tempted, but thinks about what might be on the last floor, so up she goes.

Floor 6 – The sign says: You are visitor 29, 675, 321 to this floor. There are no men on this floor. This floor exists to prove that women are impossible to please. Take the stairs down and thank you for shopping at the husband store.

Across the street, a store has opened that sells new wives. This store has the same rules as the husband store. A man goes into the wife store to find a wife.

Floor 1 – The sign says: This floor has wives that love sex.

Floor 2 – The sign says: This floor has wives that love sex, have a job, and like beer.

Floors 3, 4, 5, or 6 have never been visited.

Most people would agree the story has some truth to it and illustrates one difference between men and women.

Return Policy

A store to find a husband or a wife sounds like a good idea, but similar problems occur with or without a store when selecting a mate. Do the 'spouse' stores have a return policy? Are there cash refunds or exchanges only? What can you do if the merchandise is damaged? Do spouses come with a guarantee? Is there truth in advertising? Is it buyer beware? Is there a lay-away plan? Can you charge your item? What is the life expectancy? Is there built-in obsolescence? What are the maintenance costs? Can you trade in for a new model every few years? In other words, all the same issues and problems that come with any mate acquisition procedure are still there. There is no easy answer, no short cut to finding your one and only. Mating is not an issue. Finding a mate that you want to keep or a mate that wants to keep you is the issue.

Romance Advice

After decades of romance advice from counselors, magazine writers, relationship websites, couples trainers, sociologist's surveys, and marriage gurus, a plan or happiness formula should be available for all the Bobs and Bettys in the country. You can search the internet and find thousands of suggestions for a healthy relationship and lasting marriage. Yet we have a 50% divorce rate in the US and that does not count the ones who stay married because of finances, fear, or family pressure. These gurus skip the most important part of the success formula; much of our behavior is GENETICALLY controlled. The 'secret' to a long term relationship is both 'nature' and 'nurture'. Sociologists deal in conscious behavior (nurture). Your genetic code deals in unconscious behavior (nature). If you recall the twin studies, our genome may control 50% to 70% of our behavior and our reactions to other people. Bob and Betty, Carl and Carol, John and Jane must be on the same 'wave length' or more specifically, the same 'genetic wave length' before the move to nurture and a lasting relationship can take place.

Finding a mate is like a jig-saw puzzle; pieces have to fit together or the picture is not complete. Finding a long term mate takes several matching puzzle pieces both genetic (nature) and behavioral (nurture). Mating for the long term takes a keen sense of selectivity. Let's look at the genetic pieces first. Matching sympathetic genomes is the essential first step to a lasting relationship.

GENETIC EFFECTS

Attraction is Not a Choice

The first thing we know from nature is that attraction is not a conscious act. Our initial reaction to another person is genetically determined. Somewhere in our own particular design our senses react to our environment. Our genes determine when, where and how much or how many hormones will be released. It is not enough that Betty's genome is triggering hormones; Bob's genome must also be triggering similar hormones if there is to be a match. The human dilemma is that there are thousands of various gene formulas among the Bobs and Bettys of the world so confusing signals are being sent and received. Pheromones appear to be gene specific. That is certain males will be attracted to a specific female pheromone (matching chemistry) and vice versa. Go to any social function and watch people gravitate to some but not others. In today's terms, the 'Wi-Fi' is on, but do you have the password?

The First Connection

When we talk about two people having certain chemistry, it really is the chemistry of hormones and pheromones. When the chemicals hit the receptors, the brain reacts in many ways. There are subtle signs that chemistry is at play and messing with your actions and perceptions. Have you ever seen and smelled somebody and had your breath taken away? As mentioned in chapter 11, experiencing a feeling of familiarity is a sure sign of chemistry at work and an essential first step of the mating puzzle.

The Vibe – Another Genetic Puzzle Piece

There is another factor in humans that will insure a constant mating urge. We call it a 'vibe', a little electricity that tingles up and down one's spine. As it turns out, humans are electro-neural beings. Our nervous system sends electric signals throughout our body with messages for action. From the field of quantum physics comes the idea that we have our own specific electric charge from the atoms that make up our bodies. It seems each person may have his or her own signature vibe. Sometimes a touch may seem magical and ignite that electrical vibe. With some, one can see the sparks really fly. Those tingles are real, and another love piece begins to fit.

The Eye of the Beholder

We know that some people turn us on and some people do not. Not all beautiful people are beautiful to everyone. Beauty is not really in the eye, but in the genes. What makes your glands produce those pheromones or oxytocin is determined by your genetic code. Sights and colors must set off some triggers, as evidenced by the brightly colored males strutting around the animal kingdom. Sounds, smells, and touch provide more stimuli for the brain. Taste, by association, can set off certain triggers associated with love/sex. A woman eating a chocolate covered strawberry, sipping on a flute of champagne offered to her by a man focused on her happiness can overcome a mental hesitation as the aphrodisiac kicks in. There are a few other tastes and smells that have been shown to provide some aphrodisiac effects. While chocolate is the most famous, garlic has been shown to stimulate blood flow. Many spices produce hot, racy feelings that may translate into a personal hot, racy feeling. Top dinner or a movie off with some 'Good and Plenty' candy. Licorice scent is famous for an increase in amorous feelings, even 10 times more effective than perfume. Sensory perception is felt in the brain. The brain really is the largest sex organ in the body.

One survey I read years ago asked at which date sex occurred. The consensus was the third date. It seemed if the first date went well enough, then there would be a second date. One survey noted that 66% of people decide in the first half hour if there will be a second date. 13% of people simply walked out on the first date. The second date is a crucial date. If all the triggers are still firing then a third date would be the tipping point for getting to the 'on ramp' or getting to the 'off ramp'. No doubt, if freedom of thought is available, sex may be on the table (no pun intended) on the third date. Sex may occur on the first date, or the sixth or seventh date which makes the average the third date. This is perhaps the first check point on our "is he/she the one" check list. If you have gone eight or nine dates with no sex, then she is not really into you and is just lonely or terribly insecure or inhibited. Sex and mating urges are the nature of things. Sex is a vital link to the future relationship. No sex means no genome match and it is best to move on. (The over 50 group will have a different time table.)

There is another concern to be addressed at this level also. The question is, are you overlooking some annoying habits just to have sex? This goes for either partner, man or woman. That is okay if you have decided the relationship is going to end at the sex level, and you feel comfortable with that end in mind. This approach may not be fair to the other person, but sexual urges often overcome sensible decisions.

Friends First

Essentially there are two ways to match genomes. One is the initial attraction between the complimentary genetic systems. The other is the 'friends first' and the effect of proximity that slowly puts the genetic systems in synchrony. If the initial meeting does not produce the mutual, sympathetic, harmonious genetic reaction that triggers that feeling of lust, a continued presence may set rhythms in synchronization instead. Working together, meeting with mutual friends, being in the same club, close proximity, etc. may help align those mutual codes. Characteristics that were not readily apparent may come to light. One day you realize you look forward to seeing your 'friend', and are a little sad if he/she does not appear. With any attraction between two people, time will tell. In one study, two-thirds of people report they fell in love with someone they have known for some time versus someone they just meet. Couples' personalities converge over time. Unconsciously, the path is free of annoying habits or visual dead ends, which will allow romantic feelings to grow. There is no rush to get this person to bed, so no reason to overlook eventual obstacles. The sexual heat may rise slowly, but that is okay. When it hits, it will growl with passion.

Long Distance Romances

Long distance romances do not usually work. The sensory triggers that send stimulants to the romantic reward center are no longer present. The mind and body forget what happened. The reminders are gone. The sensory directives that initiated the love process are gone. Groping and screwing are gone. Proximity is gone. Plus, other sensory stimulators are circling around your long-distance loved one, and the genetic, biological mandates take over. You get horny, and sexual demands take over. A month, two months max, and the romance is over.

Different Wave Length

An unfortunate corollary to falling in love is that you cannot make someone fall in love with you if your codes are different. It is like trying to tune into a radio station without an antenna. It is like trying to get an AM station with an FM receiver. Do you remember all those times you liked someone but they didn't like you? And the reverse, when someone liked you but you didn't like them? It seemed you were out of sync with the romance matrix. That is exactly what I am talking about; codes that are not 'Sympatico'. Even being slightly out of synchronization means feelings from each are not going to happen together. You might feel a 'vibe' but have no chemistry, or you may like what you see, but have no sparks. The sex might be exciting, but if the next morning is bland, then enjoy the sex but do not make any long-range plans. You can try flowers, cards, delicious meals, a trinket or two, but in the long-run someone is going to be disappointed and hurt.

Negative Triggers

While not all women and men react the same way to the same visual stimulus, there seems to be some visuals, on first sight, that shut down any further interest. While clothes may make the man, there are some 'looks' that women react to with an "ugh". Evidently, according to surveys taken by women, clothes may break the man. Women generally pay a lot of attention (and time and money) to the way they look, and so are attuned to style and choices. A few of the male fashion faux pas listed by women that may be immediate turn offs are: novelty belt buckles, high-waisted pants, short pant legs (high waters), baggy/saggy pants, tube socks, socks with sandals, crocs, speedos, collar up on polo shirts, Hawaiian shirts, belly packs, torn off sleeves, cutoff jeans, and wearing more jewelry than women. In a category all by itself are men or women who try to dress like something they are not; cowboys, rappers, hippies, models, movie stars, and jocks to name a few. It is not so much the wrong look that is questionable, but it is about the mental process that thought that look was appealing. Some critics even link the man's wardrobe 'scruff' to laziness and bad manners. As with anything these days, help can be found on the internet. Numerous 'menswear blogs' have shown up on line. Other critics note that men can still be divided into urban vs. rural and white collar vs. blue collar. They say you cannot tell a book by its cover, but these outward styles give a female a glimpse of what is inside or not inside.

Hygiene

Along with shape and fashion clues there are other items that set off negative triggers. Dirt and black heads are usually a turn off. Too much make-up, yellow teeth, and wrinkled, and smelly clothes often indicate a lack of concern for health and self. Bad breath (yuck mouth), body odor or too much cologne, and sticky hair (nose hair) generally light up the 'no further interest' sign. The biological imperative of producing healthy offspring will shut down any feeling of sexual desire if the mate looks unhealthy.

Voice

If the initial look goes well, the next sense contacted is the voice. The voice can be a huge turn on. The ear is acutely aware of melody. Singers draw huge crowds of adoring fans. A sexy, female voice will melt any man in his tracks. Sharp, high pitched voices scar the ears. A good laughing voice by a man or a woman will trigger pleasant and hopeful feelings. Women love a deep male voice. A man speaking out of his nose will not woo many women. What people want to hear is a good, strong, confident voice; that is very appealing. I read where a company will (for a moderate cost) analyze the voice patterns of your prospective mate or partner for negative or positive characteristics. You tape a conversation with your friend, ask questions and the analysis will reveal if they are lying to you or not. Apparently sincerity may be detected in your voice. I suppose a possible mate might be put off by taking a lie detector test but if you cannot trust your own personal genetic detection system you might want to hire an outside source.

Sense of Smell

Odor detecting plays a huge part in the genetic reception of finding a mate. The human nose has about 5 million olfactory receptors. These are microscopic proteins that allow us to detect odors. Humans do not have the olfactory sense of other animals but we are still genetically fixed to sniff out a desirable mate. Cats have as many as 80 million receptors, while dogs have as many as 300 million receptors. It is probably a good thing humans are limited in odor detecting; the wrong odor certainly shuts down my libido. I am reminded of a movie I saw back in the '70s called "A Boy and His Dog". The movie takes place in the future after some earth destruction event. Men and dogs bond together in a mutually helpful partnership. Dogs can no longer sniff out food, a bonded man must feed the dog to which he is bonded. The dog, in turn, can sniff out women, so in return for the food, the dog leads the man to a woman. There are not enough women or dogs to go around, so there is quite a competition for dogs and women. It is kind of a dark movie, but an interesting take on olfactory senses.

Smell Desire

What drives one person into the arms of another? Can the nose influence the genitals? Scientists have long been aware that the body produces powerful air-borne chemicals called pheromones. The sex cycle of most vertebrates operate on pheromones. Humans have receptors in the nasal cavity whose sole function is to detect sexual pheromones. This detection system reports directly to the OMG center that hooks directly to the genitalia. Each individual genome has genes specifically designed to enhance the detection of a compatible mate through smell, as well as give off odors that may attract a mate. The extension of this smell design is to elicit a desire to have sexual relations when particular pheromones are detected. It is likely that females give off more pheromones than males. Nature's plan was always to let the males know when a female was in heat (ovulating) to insure successful baby-making. Women are sexiest when ovulating. This genetic disposition makes birth control precarious.

Enhanced Odors

Scientists have analyzed pheromones from many animals. We can buy yellow jacket and queen bee pheromones to put in traps; one whiff of that stuff and the little winged critters head right for the trap looking for the little lady. I am sure hundreds or thousands of scientists are trying to isolate a human sexual attractant pheromone. There are thousands of products on the market today for sale under the claim of added sexual powers or attract ability; none of them work. (Unfortunately, rhinos are being killed for their horn which is supposed to enhance sexuality.) As mentioned, the perfume industry reels in billions of dollars yearly by selling artificial pheromones. Some smells are pleasant, but according to new research a potential mate may prefer a woman's natural scent to prepared perfumes. Based on saliva samples, men were found to have higher levels of testosterone if they smelled a shirt worn by an ovulating woman. The study concluded "…that olfactory cues to female ovulation influence biological responses in men." Well duh, that has only been going on for 350 million years.

Tears for Fears

Another interesting study was done on tears and their chemical signals. There are two different kinds of tears: emotional and reflex. Reflex tears are reactions to dust or other irritants, and these tears help wash the eye. Emotional tears are, as their name implies, caused by emotions, like sadness. As crazy as it sounds, a woman's emotional tears are a turn off to men. Even though there is no discernible odor, they lower a man's testosterone level. Also, the neural networks associated with sexual arousal showed less activity around emotional tears. Further, emotional tears did not make men empathetic. And the topper is, when men sniffed emotional tears they found women less sexually attractive. This might also explain why men hate to go to 'chick flicks'. The women start sniffling, and the men, feeling their testosterone levels dropping, want to jump on a Harley, ride to a bar and shoot pool and drink beer, and hang with the guys. My wife says this reaction to tears is a good thing. If she is upset, she wants to be left alone. Plus, she hates it when I laugh during her 'chick flick."

Not Insensitive

This is a good chance to put a misconception to rest. Men are not insensitive, knuckle draggers when it comes to a crying woman. How many times is the scene played out where a woman, sniffling and teary-eyed says to the man, "You just don't care about me...you are so insensitive, boo-hoo." Well, now we know men are genetically turned off by tears, it is in our genes. We are not insensitive; in fact, our sensory organs are working perfectly.

Dogs Can Smell Cancer

I mention this for two reasons. Research shows that some cancers give off specific odors that are detectable by dogs. Perhaps other diseases, or even personality traits, might give off detectable odors; maybe a 'mean person' smell or a 'liar' smell. Wouldn't it be cool if we could give a prospective mate a breath test and view their hidden mental and physical profile based on proteins given off in their breathe? Until then, have a dog around and watch your dog's reaction to this new person. Many people do value their pet's reaction to other people. Your dog may detect an odor of an undesirable trait. They can sniff out a rat. If you are the new person meeting a pet for the first time, always carry dog treats in your pocket.

NURTURE EFFECTS

Conscious Selection

Assuming the genomes are in sync, the next piece of the mate selection puzzle is the mental/social aspect. A lasting relationship is a blend of the physical and the social (the nature and nurture). Both are equally important for a lasting relationship.

Lists

Often we create a mental list of desirable traits we want in a mate. Upon meeting a person of interest we compare our new acquaintance to that list. Our new acquaintance may rate well on initial meeting with the requisite vibe, and high ratings on the attraction meter. He or she may smell good, and look good but the lineup of wishful vehicles in the brain train can also enhance or 'de-enhance' the attraction. You might be 'hot to trot' but a miss-matched cortex search could be a mental cold shower. These lists may evolve over time and circumstance. I found the following lists on the internet. It is a little lengthy but gets the point across about the changing of desirable aspects of interest over time.

What I want in a Man, original list (age 22)

1. Handsome 2. Charming 3. Financially successful 4. A caring listener 5. Witty 6. In good shape 7. Dresses with style 8. Appreciates finer things 9. Full of thoughtful surprises.

What I want in a Man, revised list (age 32)

1. Nice looking 2. Opens car doors and holds chairs 3. Has enough money for a nice dinner 4. Listens more than talks 5. Laughs at my jokes 6. Carries bags of groceries with ease 7. Owns at least one tie 8. Appreciates a good home-cooked meal 9. Remembers birthdays and anniversaries

What I want in a man, revised list (age 42)

1. Not too ugly 2. Doesn't drive off until I'm in the car 3. Works steady and splurges on dinner out occasionally 4. Nods head when I'm talking 5. Usually remembers punch lines of jokes 6. Is in good enough shape to rearrange furniture 7. Wears a shirt that covers his stomach 8. Remembers to put toilet seat down 9. Shaves most week-ends.

What I want in a man, revised list (age 52)

1. Keeps hair in nose and ears trimmed 2. Doesn't belch or scratch in public 3. Doesn't nod off to sleep when I'm venting 4. Is in good enough shape to get off the couch on week-ends 5. Usually wears matching socks and fresh underwear 6. Appreciates a good T.V. dinner 7. Remembers your name on occasion 8. Shaves some week-ends.

What I want in a man, revised list (age 62)

1. Doesn't scare small children 2. Remembers where the bathroom is 3. Doesn't require much money for upkeep 4 Only snores lightly when asleep 5. Remembers why he is laughing 6. Is in good enough shape to stand up by himself 7. Usually wears some clothes 8. Likes soft foods 9. Remembers where he left his teeth.

What I want in a man, revised (age 72)

1. Breathing 2. Doesn't miss the toilet.

Desires do change as you get older. A man coming home was greeted by his wife in a flimsy negligee holding a rope. She cooed, "Tie me up and you can do whatever you want." So he tied her up and went golfing.

In a study a few years ago, a biological anthropologist surveyed 10,000 people around the world to find out what each wanted in a mate. Not too surprising, the men wanted young and attractive while the women wanted wealth and power. Trust and kindness were also listed but the top two wants were clearly spelled out.

Wood Chopper

My cousin from Minnesota tells me there is a certain man that some girls are looking for as mate material. After some trial and error with men, they say they should just get a 'wood chopper'. That is, a good, steady guy whom they can trust, without all the hoopla. I heard another woman say they should give the 'second tier' guys a chance. They are nice and make good husbands. Another term for a good steady guy is 'pound puppy'. So it seems that in the long run, a guy who is kind and steady is good husband material.

I have never understood why women love cats. Cats are independent, they don't listen, they don't come when you call, they like to stay out all night and when they are home they like to be left alone and sleep. In other words, every quality that women hate in a man, they love in a cat.

Right for You

One of our profound questions is, "how do I know if he/she is right for me"? I have a quiz that all men should give to a potential mate. It is a multiple choice test with a simple scoring system.

Woman's Quiz

Men, give this quiz to a potential mate.

1. You find some peanut butter in the jelly jar,

    a. You chuckle saying a little peanut butter won't hurt anything.
    b. You are annoyed but not enough to complain.
    c. You remind him how lazy he is for not cleaning his knife and hope your kids won't be like him.

2. You notice your boyfriend's bathroom is always clean,

    a. You think he is a good catch.
    b. You wonder who his house keeper is.
    c. You worry he is a neat freak.

3. Your boyfriend has signed up for a golf tournament that was on your birthday,

    a. You find out when the tournament is over and schedule a party afterward.
    b. Tell him the party is on, he will be late and you are disappointed.
    c. Insist he drop out of the tournament and give him the cold shoulder treatment.

4. You see your boyfriend's sheets are always clean,

    a. You think what a good catch he is.
    b. You wonder if another woman was there earlier.
    c. You worry he is obsessive/compulsive.

5. You see your boyfriend's laundry basket is full,

    a. You offer to do his laundry.
    b. You look to see if his whites are tinted pink or blue.
    c. You figure he is lazy and what else doesn't he do.

6. When you first meet he is well groomed and smells good,

    a. You think what a good catch he is.
    b. You wonder if it is just a put on.
    c. You think he is a phony.

7. Your boyfriend helps with the dishes,

    a. You think what a good catch he is.
    b. You wonder what he is up to.
    c. You scold him because he isn't doing the dishes the right way.

8. Your boyfriend goes to his buddy's for a beer.

    a. It's okay; you want him to have a good time.
    b. You sit up, watch the clock and yell at him when he calls.
    c. The next day you tell him what a jerk he is and grump at him for the next two days.

9. Your boyfriend takes you out to dinner and a movie of your choice,

    a. You think what a good catch.
    b. You wonder what he is up to.
    c. You think he thinks you will owe him sex but you don't.

10. Your boyfriend sleeps in on Sunday, doesn't shower and is grubby all day,

    a. You think he deserves a day to kick back.
    b. Once in while is okay as long as he does something for you.
    c. You make noise so he can't sleep; you call him a slob, piggy man and hope your kids won't be like him.

The scoring system: get one point for the 'a' answer, 2 points for the 'b' answer, and 3 points for the 'c' answer.   10 = a perfect score, marry her now.

11 – 14 = worth an engagement ring.

15 – 20 = if the sex is good keep dating.

21 to 30 = head for the door.

Do You Measure Up; Very Important Concept.

I think one key question you would have to ask yourself when searching for a mate is, "Would you date yourself?" Do you measure up to the list of characteristics you expect or want in a mate? Are you emotionally, physically and financially secure? Do you keep up your appearance, show confidence and are willing to communicate in a respectful manner? Do you expect your mate to be just like you? I have always been of the opinion that you cannot ask for something from a mate that you are not willing to give yourself.

Social Acceptance

Another deal breaker for a possible mate is his/her acceptance in a social setting. Sometimes we let other people influence our personal decisions. Often times family and religion prohibit our personal choices. Societal pressures will affect mate choices in the long run. A few quickies and short term affairs may satisfy urgent biological needs but in the long run we must find our comfort zone and that includes acceptance by family, friends and often religious affiliations. Social status, education and common interests are all part of the comfort zone. I read one opinion that according to the theory of numbers, we should date at least a dozen people before choosing a long-term partner. After seeing what is available, and what feels comfortable, the odds are better that you will select a better match for the long term.

Time and Direction

If you are past the age of 18 you know events can turn on a dime. Emotions swing. Those hot, heart-felt feelings may not last more than a couple of weeks. Yet, the brain is often overruled by feelings of love/lust. People, adult people who should know better still jump into life time commitments after only a few months with a new love interest; don't do it! People often ask, "Is this love real?" What they mean, is will this love last, or will it cycle through like so many others before? As explained in the chapter on love, 'lasting' love takes time.

This is the way nature works. Meet, mate, have offspring, rest, and repeat next season. Studies have shown humans and nature often work the same way. The urgency of sexual chemistry lasts about 7 to 9 month (the time it takes to have a baby). For some it may be 9 minutes, 9 days, or 9 weeks. That rush, that initial excitement, that ripping of clothes will then flat line. What happens after that determines what happens after that. One complete cycle of the seasons is a good time to take stock of your feelings. Anything before a year is gonads talking. You have been through birthdays, holidays, vacations and numerous celebrations. Now you have a better picture of your sweetheart, warts and all. Are your brains still in sync? Do you share the same expectations? This is when you ask your sweetheart if they want to go to the next level. This is where you decide what is next.

Get Drunk

There are manipulators out there. There are people who will try to disguise their real intentions. The actions in the frontal cortex allow people to mask their feelings to get what they want. Alcohol over comes the control of the frontal cortex. Enough booze and the true personality will come out. Happy drunks are generally happy people. Mean drunks are generally mean people. If a person blames alcohol for their errant actions, do not believe them, those are the real behaviors. The alcohol took the mask off their real feelings. People who try to use alcohol as an excuse for their actions are not to be trusted. During times of stress, those same actions will occur. As much as you wish for something to be true, you have to admit when it isn't. On the other hand, if you have a great time drinking together throughout the evening and can still get home safely, then 'cheers' and happy new year.

Drive in Traffic

Another situation that will give a glimpse into a person's personality is his/her behavior on the road. Look for aggression, patience, courtesy and reactions to other drivers. Careless and reckless driving or speeding carries over to many aspects in life. If a driver can keep his/her cool in a stressful situation then prospects for good behavior in a long term relationship are good.

The Internet

One additional avenue to the truth is the internet. Check out his/her face book page. See his/her list of friends. Do a background check on your new friend. Search police records. It is scary what is available on the internet but if in doubt, check it out.

Close the Deal

So now all the tests are complete. The lists are checked off. Compatibility seems in line. You want to take it to the next level. What do you do next? While usually it is the female who makes the move to go to the next level, the man also has a (small) hand in selecting a mate for marriage. Men like women to share an interest in their hobbies. If you are dating a sports guy and you want him to see you as a potential mate you need to know and maybe even understand the following sport terms.

Beginner level:

1. First and Ten, T.D.
2. March madness, dunk, air-ball.
3. Count is 3 and 2, R.B.I., walk, hit, Louisville slugger.
4. Par, bogey, birdie
5. Pole position, lap the field, NASCAR
6. Puck, blue line, icing
7. Penalty kick, striker, goalie

Intermediate level:

1. Long bomb, go for two, onside kick
2. Nothing but net, final 4, free throw brick
3. Two away bottom of the 9th winning run at the plate, world series
4. Off the tee, woods, irons, chip, putt
5. Triple crown, win-place-show, Churchill Downs
6. Pass line, come, hard way
7. Sprints, field events, relay
8. Downhill, slalom, Nordic combined

Expert:

1. Blitz, clip, safety, over/under
2. In the paint, 'D', zone or man to man
3. ERA, boys of summer, squeeze play
4. On side bunker, lateral hazard, FUAB
5. Flop, 4th/5th street or the turn and river, pocket pair, big slick
6. Deke, blue line 2nd line
7. Parallel bars, floor ex. high bar, horse
8. Axel, toe loop, triple quad
9. Epee, saber

Of course you may have to 'go deep' into whatever is his favorite sport.

If not a sports guy there are other guy types you may date and they include: car guys, gamers, musicians, or gun and hunter types. All guys are 'something' guys. Find out what he is and make an effort to join in or at least show some interest.

Last a Life Time

Approximately 5% of the animal kingdom mate for life; the rest are seasonal. Some 'mate for life' examples are: swans, black vultures, albatrosses, turtle doves, bald eagles, French angelfish, prairie voles, wolves and gibbons. They act as a team when hunting, and share household duties, including child services.

An interesting feature of the animals that mate for life is similarity, they look alike. The male and the female are about the same size, color, and temperament (low sexual dimorphism). The biological clue here is the more you have in common the better for the long term. Looks, color, brains, social status, goals, career, religion and even friends are some of the factors of commonality. Think about how you grew up, your neighborhood, school life, clothing styles, and daily habits. You looked at yourself in the mirror every day while growing up and became familiar with those looks. When you meet someone that is similar in looks and habits and style that person seems like an old friend and gives off a comfortable feeling for you.

An interesting example of this is meeting old friends at a high school reunion. Many marriages have resulted from meeting those old friends who have similar friends and backgrounds. According to some surveys, those marriages are doing well with lasting effects.

To make that lifelong commitment there are two questions that need a 'yes' answer. The first is, 'do we have the same destination?' That is job, children, activities, retirement, home-life, etc. If one wants to live on a boat and travel the oceans and the other is an outdoorsy type who wants a cabin in the mountains then the destinations do not match. A librarian and a traveling salesman probably won't line up well. The second question goes right to the heart of the matter; "Do I want to be part of this person's world?" and conversely "Does this person want share my world?" If you are sharing a world, there is no dominating or demanding part in sharing. Each person has a role and that role is of value to the other partner. There is no competition, only encouragement. You enjoy the similarities and differences as part of the package.

One More List

Most people are afraid to talk about details or to take a matter of fact approach toward compatibility. There are numerous dating websites and relationship advice columns that stress the value of clearly describing wants and desires and expectations of yourself and your partner. In this case you and your potential mate are going to make out your own lists. Each of you will write down who you are and what you expect from your partner. You then exchange lists and see if the other person agrees with your list. Who we think we are may not jive with what the other person sees and vice versa. It is usually a surprise to find out the other person has a different take on your take. I may think I am easy-going, only to find out the other person thinks I am a little rigid in my opinions. Therefore, you both modify those lists until you both agree to the accuracy of the lists. It is like writing a contract or a prenuptial agreement. This exercise may make or break the deal.

Some possible topics, add more if you like:

Your perceptions and expectations of yourself	Perceptions and Expectations of Mate
1. Physical appearance: Fitness, weight, exercise	———
2. Emotional balance: Baggage, controlling, insecure, Must always be right	———
3. Interests: Reading, the arts, sports, clubbing, T.V.	———

4. Career: ———
   Goals, advancement,
   classes

5. Finance: ———
   Share expenses, no debt,
   Save for retirement

6. Values: ———
   Honesty, religion,
   politics, integrity,
   Kindness

7. Conversation: ———
   Topics, jokes, share time,
   respectful

8. Future: ———
   In five years, ten,

9. How to argue, criticize: ———
   No name calling, write
   down issues

10. Marriage duties: ———
    Cooking, cleaning,
    laundry, garbage

11. Sex   ———

After this exercise you will have a very good idea if this is the right person for you. The brain must be able to lock in on behavior modes. Each year revisit your contract and modify as necessary. This openness will keep your relationship alive and current.

Use Your Brain

You need the physical triggers described earlier but it takes the brain to make it last. You need both the conscious part and the unconscious part of the brain. You need the part that stores the memories and the desires (unconscious) and the part the makes the commitment and everyday effort (conscious).

To keep a relationship going you must build memories together. Dates, events, smiles, encouragement, vacations, etc., all form positive triggers in the brain. The brain remembers and you feel good. The more memories you make, the more neural pathways of loving feelings you make. Remembering the 'good ole days' makes the fun and joy with your partner more permanent. Take a lot of pictures and put them on the wall and in albums. Take movies of happy images. Brain scans show that people who view photos of a beloved experience, show activity in the part of the brain involving cravings. Paint a room together for fun. All those things you did while courting need to continue. Those physical and sensual triggers that enhanced your feelings need to be replayed and reinforced. Continuously try to stimulate those triggers that excite one another. Continue to touch, to coo, to care, to pay attention to feelings. Create or pick 'our song,' find a favorite location and activity. Find something to joke about. Do a lot of "remember whens". The physical triggers are important, stay in shape, stay active, and stay attractive. Over half the people going through a divorce sited a great weight gain by the spouse as a key issue.

Absolutely Not

Do not take for granted everything will be good without effort. Do not assume the commitment will last a life time. You must stay attractive to your mate to keep the feelings going. Just sharing a household is not the same as sharing a love. Resentment is also an unconscious feeling until it overwhelms the conscious brain and negative feelings take over. Indifference is a marriage killer.

Heart Break Hotel

"Breaking up is hard to do," are the words to a song that anyone can relate to. If you are the one that is the 'breaker' and you have 'lost that lovin' feelin' then it is not so hard for you to break up. If you are the 'breakee' and just got dumped then heart break is real and it hurts. Really, your heart does not break but a surge of hormones will take your breath away and constrict your blood vessels and make your heart feel hurt. Your conscious and unconscious brain are still in the 'I love you mode' and the absence of your object of affection is confusing to your brain and that makes you space out. Your brain starts replaying all those wonderful times you had (positive triggers) and convinces you all over again that you are still in love and may even feel more in love than before. You project this on to the heart breaker and realize he/she has obviously made a mistake. The term for that action is 'denial'. Or you may consciously realize it is over but your unconscious brain will not let it go. Recent research suggests much of our thinking is below awareness level. We may want to walk away but we have much less control of ourselves than we think so we hang on a little longer.

Beat Yourself Up

I am talking about a break-up of an affair or even a marriage. I am not talking about an abusive situation or violence of any kind. That is a whole different story. We often make ourselves mad at the other person so we can be glad to walk away. We use self-talk such as, "Well, that person is a cold jerk or a user or player and I am lucky to have found out now before it was too late". We can make ourselves out to be a victim of foul behavior. It may be a better rationalization that we say the relationship was going nowhere and the break-up was mutual… (But we can still be friends). Any way you slice it, it is a bad deal for our feelings, and we have to get over it. One of the most famous heart break songs ever sung is by George Jones, "He stopped loving her today." In the song, the poor guy relives his love for an ex-lover over and over until the day he dies. Wow, what a waste of time; probably messed up his golf game, too. For most people an emotional break-up causes an emotional breakdown. Nothing is right; everything is wrong, up is down and down is out.

There is a Way Out

Recent brain research suggests there is a way to recover and survive a break-up. The break-up can be any disruption of a relationship or a friendship. To overcome a break-up you must change those unconscious thought patterns that created the love in the first place, (the way you fell in love is the way you are going to fall out of love). Whatever you did as a couple, don't do it anymore. Do not compare new people with the old. Go to a different restaurant. Wear different clothes. Get a haircut. Change your perfume or after shave. Listen to a different radio station. Throw away all pictures, mementos or objects that remind you of that person. You must trick your unconscious brain. Read different books, westerns or mysteries but not romance novels. Get a hobby, collect something. Watch sports on T.V. or in person. Exercise. Do not mention that person's name. Have sex with someone else. Above all, do not torture yourself with what might have been. Make that person a non-person. Whenever your brain starts to replay a memory you immediately say, "Erase the tape".

Step Programs

There are dozens of 10 step, 12 step and 5 step programs that help people change behaviors. They all involve changing thought patterns. Whether it is alcohol, diet, or surviving a break-up, the process is the same; you must consciously try to change unconscious patterns. Step number one in couples break-up is to realize the other person's unconscious brain patterns have changed and your actions, vibe, or genome messages no longer influence that other person. Even harder to swallow is now someone else's vibe, actions and genome messages will trigger the oxytocin or dopamine or euphoric feelings in your old flame (really sucks man).

Other Fish in the Sea

The encouraging fact to keep in mind is you can fall in love again. There are thousands of genomes, vibes and sensory banquets available. It will take time between loves because the brain needs time to make new neural pathways. Eventually it will happen. Each love will be different from the others for each love will have a different level of attraction and different number of triggers. Do not relive the old ones, do enjoy the new ones. One surveyed found that in a life time, women had 4 sex partners and men had 7 sex partners. That was on average so any particular person may have had many more or a few less. The point being many loves are possible and they are just as real.

When Mister Right Goes Wrong, Abusive Relationship

There is only one answer to abuse; run as fast as you can. Some people want power not affection. Abuse is about control, not about love. Shut off any emotional triggers that fire and run. Getting out of an abusive relationship is difficult, but you must go! The abuser will not change. He/she is hard wired and subconsciously trained to abuse; end of story.

Chapter 13

Marriage in the USA

A woman worries about the future until she gets married. A man never worries about the future until he gets married.

A woman marries a man expecting him to change. A man marries a woman hoping she won't change.

When women wait to get married it is called "independence". When men wait to get married it's called "fear of commitment".

A Brazilian man must pay $6,500 for saying "I don't." The couple was to be married in September of 2007, but the man called it off. The judge ruled that the man must pay for "moral and material" damages. The woman's "suffering and humiliation cannot be ignored." The fine is supposed to pay for the jilted woman's wedding costs and visits to a psychologist.

A woman asked her husband if he wanted to renew their vows. He got so excited; he thought they had expired.

In a recent poll held in the US, American men and women were asked; if they had it to do over again would they marry the same person. 80% of the men said they would; only 50% of the women said they would.

Gamophobia

Gamophobia is the fear of getting married. In some cases it is an intense fear that can cause sweats and anxiety. Only 54.1% of adults reported being married in 2010. The median age of American men at their first marriage in 1970 was 23.2 years for women, it was 20.8 years. The median age for men for their first marriage in 1990 was 26.1 years and for women, it was 23.9 years. In 2010, the age for men was 28.2 years, while for women it was 26.1 years. In Canada and Europe the median age for men and women to marry is about 2 to 4 years later than in the US. In the Middle East and where marriages are arranged, the age for men was 17, and for women 15. These numbers are median ages, so just as many people were older and just as many people were younger. People from rural areas tend to marry at a younger age, while those from urban areas wed later. In the US, you can see there is a definite trend to wait longer before getting married. Traditionally it is the man who asks the woman to marry. That trend seems to be changing in the US.

Why Wait?

One divorce statistic that says your chances of getting a divorce are three times greater if you marry before age 27. Waiting to marry someone who is more mature and more financially secure is a good combination for a successful marriage.

Wedding Costs in the US

In the Parade magazine of May 2011, the following numbers were printed. The average cost of an engagement ring was $5,392.00. The average amount spent on a wedding dress was $1099.00. The average cost of a wedding was $26,984.00. 2.1 million marriages took place in 2009. In April, 2016, The Arizona Republic printed a story about wedding costs in Phoenix. The information came from 'The Knot'. Average costs of the wedding were $29,948, an increase of $2964 from 2010. The average age for the groom was 31 and 29 for the bride. Average cost of the engagement ring was $5871; wedding dress was $1469, plus accessories at $297, and hair styling at $144.

I found a question in a 'Dear Betty/Amy/Abby/etc. column. Question: 'Is there any way to calculate the odds a marriage will last'? Answer: Social scientists have made a number of attempts to predict which couples will stay together. The most recent study tracked 2,482 married or cohabiting couples in Australia over six years. It found relationships are twice as likely to dissolve when the man is more than nine years older than the women or younger than 25 when he marries or moves in. Couples who have babies before they commit or who have children from previous relationships split more often. They tend to part ways if the woman wants a child more than the man, if the woman drinks more, if the man or woman smokes, if the partners are on their second or third marriage, or if the man is unemployed. This goes back to chapter 11 when I mentioned the more you have in common, the better your chances of survival.

Kids Say the Funniest Things

It is always humorous to ask kids questions about adult activities. Books, TV shows and jokes featuring remarks by kids spring up often. The following was found on the internet with no mention of the origin.

How do you decide whom to marry?

> You got to find somebody who likes the same stuff. Like, if you like sports, she should like it that you like sports, and she should keep the chips and dip coming.
>
> – Alan, age 10

No person really decides before they grow up who they're going to marry. God decides it all way before, and you get to find out later who you are stuck with. – Kristen, age 10

What is the right age to get married?

> 23 is the best age because you know the person FOREVER by then.
>
> – Camille, age 10

What do most people do on a date?

Dates are for having fun, and people should use them to get to know each other. Even boys have something to say if you listen long enough.

– Lynnette, age 8

On the first date they just tell each other lies and that usually gets them interested enough to go on a second date.

– Martin, age 10

When is it OK to kiss someone?

When they are rich.

– Pam, age 7

The law says you have to be eighteen, so I wouldn't want to mess with that.

– Curt, age 7

The rule goes something like this: if you kiss someone, then you should marry them and have kids with them. It's the right thing to do.

– Howard, age 8

Is it better to be single or married?

It is better for girls to be single but not boys. Boys need someone to clean up after them.

– Anita, age 9

How would you make a marriage work?

Tell your wife that she looks pretty even if she looks like a truck.

– Ricky, age 10

Other comments found on the internet. I have no idea who first said them; I am just repeating what is common knowledge.

1. The trouble with some women is they get all excited about nothing, and then they marry him.

2. A man in love is incomplete until he is married. After that he is finished.

3. Getting married is a lot like getting into a tub of hot water. After you get used to it, it ain't so hot.

4. Getting married for sex is like buying a 747 for the free peanuts.

5. Wife to husband, "That's a nice shirt; I must have bought it for you."

Universal Humor

Many jokes are either a play on words (a pun) or an aspect of a cultural tradition. Few topics are universal in appeal. However, there are probably more jokes about husbands and wives, and marriage in general, than any other subject. Interactions between husbands and wives are universally humorous. Recently, the oldest joke in history was found. It was in 1900 BCE in an old Sumerian proverb from ancient Babylonia and the joke was about a young woman and her husband. The rough translation is, "Something which has never occurred since time immemorial; a young woman did not fart in her husband's lap." Evidently that was a common enough occurrence thousands of years ago that it made the joke hit parade. Most jokes are told if there is a stereotypical behavior, action, or event. Husbands, wives, and in-law's behaviors have become so predictable over the centuries that most people can relate to jokes about their behaviors. (Interestingly, one rarely hears jokes about a father-in-law. I guess they are not joke worthy.) There are many forms and configurations of marriage throughout the world, but as long as there has been some sort of male/female pair bond, there is ample opportunity for humor.

Men say they will never be able to understand women. How can women pour boiling hot wax on their upper thigh, rip the hair out by the roots and still be afraid of a spider?

Gender

I think it is logical to say the development of the Y chromosome (350 million years ago) got us to where we are today. The male role has evolved over the past 350 million years to our present day form. The fact that only males inherit a Y chromosome, and only females inherit two X chromosomes means, each gender inherits gender-based information. There is evidence the Y chromosome is getting smaller, with fewer and fewer genes. That might mean men are getting more man-like and less flexible. Conversely, the X chromosome maybe getting larger and developing more genes, and women are getting more complex. Men and women are still evolving.

Women's Liberation

The woman's liberation movement of the 60's began the gender role shift. A 2007 report tells us that for the first time in history more women than men are earning a college degree. More women than men are graduating from law school. In 1970, only 4% of husbands had wives that earned more money than they earned. In 2007, 22% of husbands had wives that earned more money than they earned.

Gender Expectations

Role reversal or not, men still act like men, and that is not likely to change. There is a joke about a transcontinental train ride that illustrates expected roles. A single man and a single woman were accidentally assigned to a sleeper car together. The woman says, "Look, its late, I'm tired. We can share the car tonight and get this straightened out tomorrow morning. You take the top bunk, and I'll take the bottom." He agrees, takes the top bunk, and she curls in to the bottom one. About one in the morning, the man leans down to the lower bunk and shakes the woman on the shoulder. He tells her he is cold and asks if she would go to the closet and get him a blanket. She says, "How about for tonight, let's pretend we are married." Wow he thinks, he can get warm and get lucky at the same time. He says, "Sure". She says, "Good, get your own fricking blanket". This joke points out expected gender roles. The woman assigns the sleeping places and takes the more convenient one; the man does not question her choice. Then the man assumes the woman will get up and do his bidding. Next, he assumes being married means sex. Finally, the woman feels that being married means she no longer has to please him. This is a role reversal from a single woman to being a wife.

Sex Education

The following is an actual extract from a sex education school text for girls, printed in the early 1960's in the UK.

"When retiring to the bedroom, prepare yourself for bed as promptly as possible. Whilst feminine hygiene is of utmost importance, your tired husband does not want to queue for the bathroom, as he would have to for his train. But remember to look your best when going to bed. Try to achieve a look that is welcoming without being obvious. If you need to apply face-cream or hair rollers, wait until he is asleep, as this can be shocking to a man last thing at night. When it comes to the possibility of intimate relations with your husband, it is important to remember your marriage vows, and in particular, your commitment to obey him.

If he feels that he needs sleep immediately then so be it. In all things be led by your husband's wishes; do not pressure him in any way to stimulate intimacy. Should your husband suggest congress then agree humbly all the while being mindful that a man's satisfaction is more important than a woman's. When he reaches his moment of fulfillment a small moan from yourself is encouraging to him and quite sufficient to indicate any enjoyment that you may have had.

Should your husband suggest any of the more unusual practices be obedient and uncomplaining but register any reluctance by remaining silent. It is likely that your husband will then fall promptly asleep so adjust your clothing, freshen up and apply your night-time face and hair care products. You may then set the alarm so that you can arise shortly before him in the morning. This will enable you to have his morning cup of tea ready when he awakes."

Like I said in the beginning, this was early 60's, so gender roles were 'traditional'. In a survey in 2011, up to 80% of women admitted to faking orgasms to speed up their partners ejaculation because they were bored, tired, or in a rush. 87% of women said they exaggerate pleasure with moans and vocal exclamations because they want to be nice and boost their partner's self-esteem.

Man Cave

Lately, men have become revolting....maybe 'rebellious' is a better term. Women have ruled the house for decades, and men have been sent to the garage to do man stuff. But that is changing. "Where is the "man room", has been the latest call from men. Men are trying to carve out their own space in the house. No flowers, no doilies, no pink, no skirts, just 'man stuff'. A keg-a-rater, pool table, big screen TV, and a foos ball table, for starters. A place to keep trophies, fishing gear, beer mugs, men's mags, Xbox and games, even a bear skin rug, is what men want. It is not an invasion of the female domain, it is reclaiming lost land. Men can put their feet up on the coffee table or lie down on the couch. They can have their buddies come over, watch sports and eat chips and dip and not worry about spilling on the living room rug or bothering the women folk. "We aren't going to the local tavern with women trying to pick us up. We are staying home in our 'man room' or 'man cave' men say." Let 'the man' be a man, at least in his own place, is the plea. Men have to suck-it-up at work and when dealing with women, so please let 'the man' and his Y chromosome have a free zone to relax.

Communication

Communication is the mother of all break downs in the male/female arena. Studies have shown that genders hear differently and process information differently. There is a line in a popular song right now that goes, "Just because I said it, doesn't mean I meant it." Women usually know what they mean when they say something; it is just that men don't understand the feminine definition of the words they are using. It is truly amazing how many definitions or meanings there are for the same word.

Womanese

Men must be able to recognize the underlying meaning of a few basic words of 'Womanese'. From the website of clean jokes come the following definitions.

Fine – I am right. This argument is over. You need to shut up.

That's Okay – One of the most dangerous statements a woman can make. "That's Okay" means she wants to think long and hard before deciding when and how you will pay for your mistake.

Nothing – The calm before the storm and you had better be on your toes. Note: Arguments that start with "Nothing" usually end with "Fine."

Go Ahead – (the butthead is silent) This is a dare, not permission.

Thanks – A woman is thanking you. Do not question this or faint. Just say, "You are welcome" and let it go.

Selective Hearing is Another Complaint
both Sexes have in Common.

A man and his wife were sitting outside one night on the porch drinking beer and he said, "I love you." The wife asked if that was him or his beer talking? He said, "It was me talking to my beer."

While attending a marriage seminar dealing with communication, Mike and his wife Mary Jane listened to the instructor. "It is essential that a husband and wife know each other's likes and dislikes." He asked Mike, "Can you name your wife's favorite flower?" "Sure", he says, looking at his wife, "Pillsbury, isn't it?" (Man still clueless.)

Husband to wife, "If something I said can be interpreted two ways and one of the ways makes you sad or angry, then I meant the other one."

A woman always has the last word in any argument. Anything a man says after that is the beginning of a new argument.

"I never mind my wife having the last word. In
fact I'm delighted when she finally gets to it."

Walter Matthau

What Every Man Wants Women to Know

Sometimes men have simple wants. We like to get along with women and we really don't want to argue. The male mind is not complex. Many of life's little bumps really are 'little' bumps.

A. Sunday sports, it's like the full moon or changing of the tides, let it be.
B. 'Yes' and 'no' are perfectly good answers to almost every question, explanations are not always necessary.

C. Whenever possible, please say whatever is on your mind during the commercials.

A man asked his girlfriend if she was sexually satisfied, and she wondered why he was so preoccupied with performance. Next time he did not ask her, and she said he didn't care about her needs.

What He Says, What He Means

"It's a guy thing", means: There is no rational pattern and you have no chance of finding one.

"It would take too long to explain," means: I have no idea either.

"Take a break honey; you're working too hard", means: I can't hear the game over the vacuum cleaner.

"That's interesting, dear," means: Are you still talking?

"Honey, we don't need material things to prove our love", means: I forgot our anniversary.

"You look terrific in that outfit," means: Please don't try on another outfit, I'm starving.

"I don't need to read the directions," means: I am perfectly capable of screwing it up without help.

Man Facts Women Should Know

Men like things women don't. Men like cartoons, action movies, motorcycles, sports, firearms, the Three Stooges, and ESPN. They do not like woman's entertainment, 'chick flicks'. However, a man will watch a 'chick flick' for sex.

When women say they want to sit down and talk, men hear, "I'm pissed." Men know they do not want to sit and talk about sports or man stuff, so telling us you want to talk means you want to bring up something that bothers you.

Domestic Gripes, The Male Brain, The Female Brain

An English teacher wrote the words: 'Woman without her man is nothing' on the blackboard, and asked the students to punctuate so it made sense. The men wrote: ''Woman, without her man, is nothing ''. The women wrote: "Woman! Without her, man is nothing. ''

A married man should forget his mistakes. There is no use in two people remembering the same thing.

"Cash, check or charge?" the cashier asked as he put her items in a bag. As she fumbled with her wallet the cashier noticed a television remote in the lady's purse. "Do you always carry a T.V. remote in your purse," he asked. "No," she replied, "but my husband refused to come shopping with me and I figured this was the most evil thing I could do to him legally."

Rejection in Bagdad

Headlines from a story in my local paper a little while ago; "Rejected as boyfriends, young men sometimes plant bombs at the girl's house." It goes like this: boy meets girl. They exchange glances and text messages. Boy asks father for girl's hand in marriage. Father says "no." Boy plants a bomb at the door. Another time a guy shot up the girl's house. So far, no one has been killed. The Middle East seems to have a different mindset when it comes to affairs of the heart.

Class Will Soon Be In Session

A man is stopped by police around 1 a.m. and is asked where he going. The man replies, "I am going to a lecture about alcohol abuse and the effects it has on the human body." The officer then asks, "Really? Who is giving that lecture at this time of night?" The man replies, "My wife."

A bride was escorted down the aisle and when she reached the altar, the groom was standing there with his golf clubs. She said, "What are your golf clubs doing here?" He looked right in the eye and said, "This isn't going to take all day, is it?"

Women will never be equal to men until they can walk down the street with a bald head and a beer gut and still think they are sexy.

A man's idea of helping with housework is to lift his leg so his wife can vacuum.

Men do not like to do housework because you make the bed, you do the dishes and six months later you have to start all over again.

What do we instantly know about a well-dressed man? His wife is good at picking out his clothes.

What is the difference between a man and childbirth? One can be terribly painful and sometimes almost unbearable while the other is just having a baby.

When a woman makes a fool of a man, it is usually an improvement.

A woman's rule of thumb: If it has tires or testicles, it is going to be trouble.

Sometimes the question comes about what is more painful, having a baby or getting kicked in the testicles (nuts)? A year after having a baby, a woman may contemplate having another baby. A year after having been kicked in the nuts, no man has ever contemplated getting kicked again. So......

Making the Marriage Last; Use Your Head

Researchers in animal behavior have long known that monogamy is not natural. It is not natural in the animal kingdom and it is not natural in the human kingdom. Homo sapiens carry the evolutionary stigmata of a mildly polygamous mammal, in which both sexes have a penchant for multiple mates bonding. However, there are a few

113

genes making their way to humans that understand the benefits of two parents helping rear a child. Human beings are also hard-wired for traits that can be used to strengthen monogamy. Hormones, like oxytocin and vasopressin, which relate to sexual satisfaction, promote a reward mechanism when interacting with the same person. Add this to the fact that people have a large brain and are able to have conscious thought. People who study primates note a strong family and social trend in the actions of primates. So we know those social/family genes are wired into the human genome. Reward mechanisms favorable to family, offspring and mates give encouragement that the human genome is trending to extended mate bonding that will last more than one season.

Making any relationship between two people work takes a lot of mental effort. Gender differences considered, a husband and wife must make a conscious effort almost daily to reinforcing the marital bond. Saying I love you and thank you often, works wonders. The 'conscious' brain must be trained, must make new neural memory pathways. In many cases, the conscious brain must overcome the subconscious training of looking for a new mate. Eventually the conscious brain, with its training, will override the subconscious brain and a permanent 'love bond' is formed.

How to Live Happily Ever After

A Valentine's special report in the USA Weekend magazine, 2011, quoted many famous spouses and romance experts. Following are some of the quotes: …

"If you can't laugh about it, it's never going to work. Also, liking each other is key to keeping passion burning."

– Nora Roberts

"Plan for the day after the wedding because that is when life together begins. Talk about how you're going to live together: in-laws, kids, geography, religion, sex and division of labor. If you have the same expectations, OK. If not, you have to negotiate a middle ground."

— Phil McGraw, aka Dr. Phil.

"Treat the person you care most about the same way you treat them on Valentine's Day. I'm not talking about flowers or candy. I'm talking about something much deeper: having affection and respect, and sharing and communicating."

— Jeanne Phillips, aka Dear Abby

"Don't sweat the small stuff and focus on the positive. And the sooner you learn to say 'Yes Dear' the better it is."

— Spike Lee

"Slow down! Say little things every day to show you care, whether it's saying 'I love you', tucking a note in their lunch or giving them a compliment. Studies show this makes a significant impact on whether a couple will stay together."

— Terri Orbuch, aka The Love Doctor

"Respect for each other, patience to build a life together and taking care of each other emotionally and physically are the base upon which lasting love is built."

— Vera Wang

"Don't say the first thing that comes to mind. People tend to forget the person they live with deserves as much respect as someone they work with, if not more."

— Cokie Roberts

"Develop a marriage mission statement, such as 'We're going to have two children, we'll be totally faithful, and we'll make sure our children are raised in an environment of love, respect and synergy."

— Stephen R. Covey

"At least twice weekly, commit to 30 minutes of kissing and cuddling without a TV on. And don't let more than two weeks go without sex…."

— Laura Berman

More Advice

You can find advice on any subject when searching the internet. There is no shortage of experts on relationships. It seems much of the advice for married people should have been discussed pre-marriage. Once locked into a marriage, it is difficult to face opposing or unexpected ideas and attitudes. The following tips are condensed from several articles found on the internet, magazines and newspapers.

Love Your Spouse First

Over the past decade or two, children have been elevated to the number one concern for many parents, especially mothers. Experts warn against this move. Too many children these days, experts say, are growing up with an 'entitlement' attitude. Kids are expecting to be given anything they want without really earning their privileges. The collateral damage is that husbands are being 'shelved' or considered second to the child by the wife/mother. This is especially true in 'blended' families and remarriages.

Many experts say taking care of your spouse is the number one priority for a lasting marriage.

If mom and dad aren't happy, then the kids won't be happy. Too often, the kids grow up, move out, and the parents find they have nothing in common (the empty nest syndrome). Romantic love and kid love are two different things. Kids who watch their parents caring for each other learn a healthy respect for love and affection.

Picking the Partner

Finding someone good is not about finding someone 'hot' or 'rich' or without faults, it's about finding someone whose strengths elevate you. Look for a partner who makes your life more interesting. Research shows the more self-expansion you experience from your partner the more satisfaction is found in the relationship. Has being with your partner resulted in learning new things, or made you a better person?

Find a mix of individuality and teamwork. Let yourself be influenced by your partner. Men are more resistant to being influenced by women, but the goal should be an equal exchange of ideas in the marriage.

Each partner brings something to the table and those behaviors become an essential part of the whole relationship. ***Is your partner making you a better person?***

Responding positively to your partner's success gives him/her a boost. Do not be jealous. Giving support during a loss shows genuine concern. Say, "I love you" every day. Do not be emotionally stingy with your partner.

You should like your partner as well as love him/her.

Make an effort to be well-mannered and attractive to your partner. Do not take caring or romance for granted.

Arguments/ Disagreements

Disagreements are inevitable. Whenever a man and a woman share a space, boundaries will be crossed, frustration and hurt feelings will occur and heads will butt. Negotiating is essential to avoid alienation and anger. As always, your attitude may tip the balance toward a good or bad outcome. Try to remember, you are both on the same team. Here are more tips and advice from the experts.

Be willing to forfeit, do not become polarized in your disagreement, there is rarely only a 'right' or 'wrong' in an argument.

Get to the point, nicely. Be direct, indirect communication can be damaging. Find a way to discuss touchy subjects. A combative approach rarely works.

Do not argue late at night when you are tired and less emotionally articulate. If an issue is not resolved, agree to put it aside, get some sleep, and take it up later.

Disagreements over money are a leading cause of divorce. Talk in terms of 'ours'. The saver does the budget; the spender is in charge of celebrations and pizza toppings.

The most important aspect of arguing is the ability to say, "I'm sorry". Apologizing takes the hostility out of the argument. Of course the flip side to that is accepting the apology. Once that happens, the subject is forgotten, never to arise again.

There are several make-or-break events or problems that arise in any marriage. Job loss, sickness, children, relocation, and death are a few of those problems. Experts tell us it is not the problem that matters but how each person will deal with it that counts. As a couple you are a team, seeking a team approach, both people working together, to handle a problem works the best. Blaming one another never works.

Signs You are Lasting

Watch any two people who like each other and you will see a lot of mirroring. After enough time, their faces will be in sync. That is, they will smile together, nod together, express the same feeling together and seem to look alike. You might hear someone say, "You are such a cute couple".

Over time, personal gains from a lasting relationship blend into each person. Research suggests that spouses eventually adopt the traits of the other. Activities, traits, behaviors become common ground and are an essential part of how each person experiences life.

It is easy to agree with the advice from the 'experts', it is harder to actually follow the advice. At the very least, one can use this information as a general outline or reality check.

Love American Style

The following information comes from a survey AARP did in 2009. 2000 Americans from ages 18 to 65-plus were asked several questions about love. Americans were compared to a recent survey of French citizens and their answers concerning love. The results are very interesting considering the stereotypic attitudes of the French and Americans. The French love romance, poetry, and candle-lit dinners and the Americans are red-and-white-and-prude fuddy-duddies. The French hold each other, and Americans hold the remote. The results from the respondents ages 50 to 64 are: 75% of Americans believe they have encountered the love of their life. 81% of the French felt that way. 80% of Americans say it's not likely they would leave their mate. 67% of the French felt the same way. 30% of Americans felt they could fall head over heels in love. Only22% of the French felt that way. 15% of Americans are willing to alienate family and friends for love. 23% of the French would do it.

It seems the biggest difference between the French and Americans revolves around sex. The French lifestyle is slower and more sensual. The French allow time in their lives for sex and playfulness. American attitudes in relationships are more about stability than sack time. Brain scans of people in long-term relationships showed increased activity in an area associated with calm, but none in an area associated with anxiety. (Maybe that is why married folk live longer.) Brain scans also show that love spurs the body to produce dopamine (a natural stimulant) whether you are 18 or 80, in a new or long-term relationship.

There was a big explosion at the job site and a middle-aged man was rushed to the hospital unconscious. When he awoke, the doctor was there and explained what had happened. "I have some bad news and some good news for you," the doctor said. "As a result of the explosion, your penis was blown off, but the good news is we can rebuild it just as good as new, if not better. You have a 9,000 dollar cash benefit and it costs 1,000 dollars an inch to rebuild. I do not know what your expectations are or those of your wife so you can discuss that with her tonight and I'll talk to you in the morning." The next morning the doctor arrived and asked if the man and his wife had made a decision about the 9,000 dollars. "Yes", the man said. "We talked about it quite a bit." "What did you decide to do with the 9,000 dollar benefit?" asked the doctor. "My wife decided we were getting granite countertops".

Future of the Sexes – Future of Marriage

Genes have been recently found in the primate groups that show tendencies for strong social ties and support of the immediate family members. And while men still look for young, attractive women, there appears to be happy hormone stimulants from interacting with the same spouse in a long-term relationship. Women may look first for a man who can provide creature comforts, but since many women today are taking their own lives in their hands and finding careers, security may no longer be a prime consideration in a mate. However, kindness and honesty are as important as ever. Men and women in the western world are getting married later in life and are having fewer children than was typical in their parents' generation.

Fortunately, social trending genes and pair bonding genes seem to be gaining strength in humans. It is becoming clear, however, that women are the ones who must guard the development of human relationships. That means women must understand men in order to guide them through domestic life. Men are what they are; an X and Y chromosome. They have not changed in 30,000 years and there is no indication that they are going to change in the future.

Marriage works for society. (That goes for any two people who wish to be a couple.) There is no doubt that children do best with two parents. The more the parents care for each other, the better the children become and the stronger the family unit becomes. The stronger the family unit, the better the society becomes.

Statistically, we know happily married people live longer and are healthier than single people. The future for marriage looks good. The key is taking your time, at least a year, with a potential mate and discussing a marriage plan before getting married. (Young love does not conquer all). A contract with expectations may sound cold and un-loving, but both people working together toward a common goal insures mutual respect, a positive attitude, and a greater chance for a lasting relationship.

In the next chapter I propose a list-writing exercise that every couple should undertake before getting married. Drafting a marriage contract, of needs and desires, opens wide the door to understanding and communication. Unlike the little girl's explanation of marriage where god decides who you get, and then later you get to see who you're stuck with; a prenuptial set of directions insures your model will stand a good chance of success.

Chapter 14

The Check list

Fairy Tales Can Come True

You meet someone special. The initial attraction is hot. You fall in love. You get married and live happily ever after. This scenario sounds like a fairy tale. With a little understanding of the opposite sex and an itemized check list your fairy tale may come true. Frank Sinatra sang a great song titled 'Young at Heart'. The words start, "Fairy tales can come true, it can happen to you, if you're young at heart". My version is, "Fairy tales can come true, it can happen to you, if you follow the check list." Navigating through love takes a guide, a check list, something to make sure you are on the right path. There are several levels in a personal relationship from the meeting to the living happily ever after. The check list provides the guide posts that will help you navigate through the decision making process of a lasting, happily-ever-after relationship.

Chapter 14 is the wrap, the 'seal the deal' check list. So the initial attraction has survived several dates, the sexual involvement is good. You have made it through the first year, all the holidays with family and the excitement is still keen. You have neutralized the little annoying habits of your partner and you are looking forward to a future with your new love.

Marriage Proposal

I think every marriage should have a pre-nuptial agreement. Essentially it is a check list of agreements with an escape clause if necessary. This way you know what the other person's expectations are in case of dissolution, and hopefully you agree with their mindset. These attitudes are an important ingredient in planning the future. Some say it means you are planning for failure, not for the future, but actually it synchronizes the marriage. If your partner refuses to discuss a dissolution process (divorce happens 50% of the time) then that should be a deal breaker. Going into a marriage, a commitment for life, you must have your eyes wide open and know what your partner is thinking.

Just getting through the wedding day is a real eye opener, and a real test of compatibility. Most brides think this is her big day, and she, and her mother, get to make all the plans. If the man is excluded from the planning of the wedding and he is good with that, then you both are already heading down the wrong path. Marriage includes a bride and a groom.

Bed, Bath and Beyond

By now you have spent a lot of time at each other's home. There should have been plenty of dinners, breakfasts, and sleep overs. You have seen how the other half lives and you have a good idea of what the future living arrangements look like. Hopefully you have discussed miscues, quirks, and differences in life styles, along with duties and responsibilities of everyday life.

One quirk I have concerns speech patterns. When I hear someone say, "Her and I went shopping…", or "Me and her went shopping…" I cringe. I taught school for over 30 years, so I spent 30 years correcting speech patterns. It may sound silly, but mistaken use of nouns and pronouns, and mistaken verb tense, give me the chills. I certainly do not correct friends in passing conversations, but I could not spend years of my life with a spouse that sent chills up my spine on a daily basis. Personal quirks are wrinkles that need to be ironed out.

You now need a final walk through before the building is complete. The more details and expectations you can nail down early the fewer hair-raising surprises occur. Of course, the rule of thumb should be to treat the other person as you want to be treated. Don't expect them to do for you what you can do for yourself. And don't expect them to do something you wouldn't't do.

Each of you take a pad of paper and go from room to room, and write down your responsibilities and expectations, desires and limits. You may think you know the other person by now, but there may still be some surprises. Swap lists when you are done and see how compatible your thoughts really are. This may sound nit-picking or unloving, but as they say, "the devil is in the details". It is better at this level to discover any deal breakers or areas in which to compromise before disagreements turn to anger. Who does the dishes, the cooking, the shopping, the paying, the planning, and the 'Bar-B-Qing'? If you are both working, then sharing the chores makes sense. Maybe you can trade cleaning for yard work for car maintenance? I know several working couples where the husband expects the wife to do all the kitchen work. Unrealistic expectations can lead to anger and divorce. Irreconcilable differences are the main cause of divorces today. Use the check list to discover those differences and reconcile now. Back in the 1950's, before no-fault divorce, one spouse had to have a reason for wanting a divorce. As strange as it may seem, and as unbelievable as it may seem, squeezing the middle of the toothpaste tube was the cause listed for divorce seven times in California. Do not waste your time growing angry; use your time sharing the wonders of life.

Most of the items on the check list probably were already addressed over the past year and most already passed muster or you would not be this far along in your relationship but it is still a good idea to cover expectations and desires openly and clearly before making a lifelong commitment to marriage. This is where those little nagging resentments must be addressed. The divorce cases involving squeezing the tooth paste tube in the middle were not really about squeezing the tube in the middle; it was about not recognizing irritations and not respecting your partner's feelings.

Passing Gas

One example of an item that may be found on a compatibility list is passing gas. On average, a human passes gas about 20 times a day. Consequently this event becomes apparent while working out living arrangements in a marriage. Men seem to announce this event in a greater volume than women. To ask your spouse to leave the room when the pressure builds is not always convenient. I knew of one woman who felt the man should either leave the room or just hold it until the feeling passed. I do not think that was the reason she already had 3 husbands and was looking for a 4th, but who knows.

Having to get up from bed several times a night to pass gas does not work well. Pretending to pass gas while asleep is not always believed. One couple I knew made an arrangement. For a new car, the wife agreed the husband could fart in bed. Some agree that one at least turn away from your spouse while passing and lift the covers to keep from trapping the gas under the blankets.

Closing doors, turning off the lights, position of the toilet paper are all minor things but ignoring your spouse's wishes becomes a major thing. Being unreasonable about living conditions is also a major annoyance to peaceful and happy living conditions. I knew one couple who went together for 7 years before they got married. 10 months after living together 24/7 they divorced. She could not stand the way he passed his day; there was no list of expectations. I knew a couple who, for 2 years, had separate quarters. The husband had his own apartment and the wife had her apartment. They loved each other but just could not live together for long. Many men I have talked to said their marriage probably would have lasted longer if they had not lived together with the wife. Marriage is amazingly convenient and inconvenient at the same time.

The List

Thinking about and talking about feelings and desires and expectations in an open conversation will settle a lot of arguments before they happen. Even discussing the rules of arguing is important. The better you know your spouse the better you can accept your spouse and the brighter your future together will be. As I mentioned, go from room to room and write down anything that comes to mind about expectations and responsibilities.

The living room may be the safest place to start. I will suggest a few things to consider but each party needs to pen their own list.

Living room: Furniture arrangement and style, room décor, cleanliness, newspapers/magazines, TV shows, remote control, sports, smoking in the house, end tables, eating in the living room.

Kitchen: Who cooks, when, clean up, dishes, sink, refrigerator, stove, menu, food likes and dislikes, how cooked, grocery shopping, budget, wine, beer, drinks, deserts, appliances, trash – who takes it out and where stored, clearing the table, which meals are common, which separate.

Bathroom: routine in morning and at bed time, shower, shave, personal hygiene, deodorant use, brush teeth, kind of toothpaste, perfumes, after shave, make-up, storage, peeing pooping alone, door open or closed, toilet paper, over or under, replace, separate towels, sinks, drawers, who cleans, how often, wipe down shower after use, shower together, naked together in am/pm, shave legs other body parts, toilet seat up or down, cover up or down, door opened or closed, skid marks in the toilet.

Bedroom: how much sex is expected or desired each week, how adventurous with sex are you, can we experiment, use toys, different positions, oral sex, talk dirty, discuss closet space, dresser space, who decorates, makes the bed, cleans, how often change the sheets, passing gas in bed, clothes on the floor, in a hamper, hanging up, TV in bedroom, reading in bed, lights out, sleeping positions, snoring, being naked, P.J.s, wardrobe, fashion sense.

House in general: clutter, dusting, vacuuming, windows, painting, floors, plumbing, cleaning gutters, repairs.

When I was a kid I had a neighbor who was a hoarder. He had stuff stacked everywhere. One day a woman showed up. Either he got married or she moved in with him. It was not long before a garbage truck showed up and a ton of stuff was hauled away. Coincidently, the man died shortly thereafter.

Den: man room, wall hangings/pictures, Playboy magazine, drinking.

A man room is not always an option, but each person needs to carve out their own space. In that space masculine, and feminine traits and décor must be allowed by the other spouse. Both people must figure out what that is to be. I have a brother-in-law who has his garage decked out in his image. He loves it out there and his wife can't mess with his stuff. She often does a 'head-shakin' at his arrangement but that is his space and she keeps quiet. In the house, she rules.

Outdoors: lawns, flowers, gardening chores, design, landscaping, pets.

Pets may be a dealer breaker. I have seen people who allow their cats to walk on the kitchen counters or dining table. That would drive me nuts. I do not want to eat off an area that mimics the bottom of a cat's foot. Cats lick their butts and dogs lick their balls and I do not want their lickers anywhere near where I eat, or sit, or sleep. Pet hair on the furniture may be a deal breaker. Allergies will also play a big part of pet acceptance.

Finances can be a deal breaker. Who pays bills, keeps bank account, spending money, own accounts, clothing allowance, car allowance, major appliances/purchases.

I have heard many women complain that their husbands seem to find money for their hobbies but there is no money for items the wife wants to buy. Separate accounts to some extent may be a solution to allowance money.

Week-ends: activities, vacations, hobbies, going out, holidays where and with whom, dance lessons, sense of humor. One of the delights of my marriage is that my wife 'lets' me exhibit my sense of humor. She does not always get it or appreciate it but I get to be me, I get to laugh a lot.

Misc.: golfing, going out with the boys/girls, bowling.

Kids: how many, what activities, child raising, discipline.

A buddy I play golf with told me of a first date he had with an attractive woman. During the evening he mentioned that he was an avid golfer and played 3 or 4 times a week. He explained about the men's club on Wednesdays and week-end games played with different friends. A little later in the conversation she mentioned that if they got together that she would 'let' him play golf once a week on Wednesdays with the men's club. That was their first and last date. Better to know expectations before commitment.

I am retired and I told my wife that I should be able to play golf three times a week. She was fine with that, but our only disagreement dealt with the weather. I do not want to play golf in the rain so I play when the sun shines. As it turns out I cannot do yard work in the rain either. When the sun shines my wife has an expectation of me getting the yard work done. If we have seven days of sunshine there is no problem. If we only have three days of sunshine and the grass is a foot high then there is a problem. My position is that the grass will still be there next week. Her position is that golf will still be there next week. Fortunately we have a couple of teen-age boys living next door and they are looking for ways to make a few bucks. In this case, money can buy happiness.

I am sure there are more items up for discussion. There is the matter of religion, politics, and education, charities, volunteer work, and more. You can make the list a game and see how many items you can list, and how many are up for discussion and how many have already been checked off. One area I mentioned in brief is rules for arguing. "Never go to bed angry" is really an over simplification of a healthy process. You may indeed need some time to puzzle over a delicate situation or adjust your view on a subject. Do agree to pick up the conversation sometime the next day, and set aside some time for honest intercourse.

That is a wrap. You now have all the info you need to know if you are in love and how to find a lifelong mate. Know full-well that environments change, people change, and sometimes you may have to walk away. Know also that life together with that special person is hard work but it is a life worth living.

The Final Thought

There is one absolute thought necessary if a marriage has a chance for success. That thought is "marriage is for life; a commitment for life."

John West grew up in Santa Monica, California. He graduated from California State University in Long Beach, California with a major in Biology, a major in Physical Education, a minor in Physical Science, and a lifetime standard teaching credential. He taught science for 33 years and retired in 2001. His science background has enabled John to give a semi-scientific bent to his humor. He has also written a children's book titled "Being Three", and recorded a CD of original cowboy poetry.

John lives 6 months on Bainbridge Island, Washington and 6 months in Scottsdale, Arizona. He is married to Valerie, has two kids, Amy and Tyler, and 5 grandsons. When he is not writing he enjoys playing golf, chainsaw carving, and cowboy fast draw competitions.

Printed in the United States
By Bookmasters

Printed in the United States
By Bookmasters